AF328904

*An Anglo-Catholic Visionary
for Modern America*

An Anglo-Catholic Visionary
for Modern America

Gordon Butler Wadhams and "The Way of Christ"

Joseph F. Byrnes

WIPF & STOCK · Eugene, Oregon

AN ANGLO-CATHOLIC VISIONARY FOR MODERN AMERICA
Gordon Butler Wadhams and "The Way of Christ"

Wipf & Stock
An Imprint of Wipf and Stock Publishers
199 W. 8th Ave., Suite 3
Eugene, OR 97401

www.wipfandstock.com

PAPERBACK ISBN: 978-1-6667-7042-1
HARDCOVER ISBN: 978-1-6667-7043-8
EBOOK ISBN: 978-1-6667-7044-5

04/05/23

To the memory of Dom Damasus Winzen, OSB (1901–1971)

Contents

1

Traditional Values and New Vision

An Introduction

THE HEADLINE ON A middle page of the April 20, 1949, edition of the *New York Times* was "6 'HIGH' CHURCHMEN BECOME CATHOLICS." The long article reports that "The Rev. Gordon B. Wadhams, who resigned on March 15 as rector of the Protestant Episcopal Church of the Resurrection at 115 East 74th Street, has been received into the Roman Catholic Church, it was learned yesterday." Subsequent paragraphs detail Wadhams's university and seminary education, previous church appointments, the simultaneous conversions of the assistant rector and several members of the congregation, reactions of members of the parish, and the role of Dom Damasus Winzen, who received him into the Catholic Church on Holy Saturday night.[1]

Gordon Butler Wadhams (1904–1987) brought to American Catholicism in the twentieth century the Anglo-Catholic values that John Henry Newman (1801–1890) brought to English Catholicism in the nineteenth century. Both of them attempted to express, historically and theologically, an orthodox Catholicism for their times, waiting for the Anglican Church or the Roman Church to conform to *that*. When they could no longer wait, they had to choose between a Roman church that demanded excessive conformity and an English church with troublesome defects where they could at least

---

1. I am grateful to Father Barry Swain, rector of the Church of the Resurrection, for providing me with a facsimile of this article.

maintain an independent existence. Both chose the Roman Church, and both of them suffered isolation, loneliness, and nostalgia to the point of tears.[2]

Gordon was born in Torrington, Connecticut, near the family home in Goshen, and spent impressionistic childhood years in Westhampton Beach, a town on Long Island's oceanside shore. His birth was reported in a 1904 issue of the *Yale Sheffield Monthly*: "A son was born January 21 to Dr. and Mrs. N. S. Wadhams. He has been named Gordon Butler Wadhams." The massive, published genealogy of the Wadhams family fills in the details on page 455! "*Noah Samuel Wadhams,* M.D., son of Francis Morris and Frances M (Palmer) Wadhams, born 27 May 1875, in Goshen, Conn.; married 17 October 1900, Eva Butler, daughter of Nathan and Almeda (Thompson) Butler. Dr. Wadhams graduated from Yale Medical College in 1900, and lives at Westhampton Beach, Long Island, N.Y. Child: Gordon Butler, b. 26 Jan., 1904."[3]

His mother's people were Episcopalians, his father's people Congregationalists. His primary schooling was in Westhampton Beach, followed by the high school years at Philips Andover Academy and college years at Yale University. Following graduation from Yale, he spent several years teaching at the Evreux lycée in northern France and the Manlius Academy in New York State and then entered the General Theological Seminary in Manhattan, from which he graduated in 1933. These are the signposts of the formation of Father Gordon Wadhams, the Episcopal priest labeled "convinced Anglo-Catholic" by his colleagues, who was rector of the Church of the Resurrection in New York City from 1936 to 1949 and served also as a homiletics instructor at General Theological Seminary across those years.

We do not have any printed records of his sermons, but we do have an invaluable record of the thought and experience that animated his preaching in the column he began more than a decade after his reception into the Roman Catholic Church. Gordon wrote warmly about his friendships with the great American Catholic reformers and innovators, Fathers Reinhold

2. For multiple relevant studies of Anglican renewals—as well as resistance to them—in Newman's nineteenth century and Wadhams's twentieth century, see Brown, *Oxford Handbook.*

3. *Wadhams Genealogy,* 455. The Wadham family had its origins in late medieval England, but firm and certain genealogical information begins with John Wadham, whose son Nicholas (1532–1609) was the founder of Wadham College at Oxford. The John Wadham who immigrated to America sometime between 1645 and 1651, settling in Wethersfield, Connecticut was from a parallel line. The "s" seems to have been added by members of the fourth generation in America. Noah Samuel Wadhams, Gordon's father, belonged to the eighth generation.

Hellriegel and Hans Reinhold and in particular with Dom Damasus Winzen OSB, founder of Mt. Saviour Monastery in upstate New York. It was Father Winzen who received him into the Catholic Church at the Connecticut monastery of Regina Laudis on Easter Sunday, 1949. He was re-ordained in 1952 by Bishop Henry J. O'Brien after three years at St. Mary's Seminary, Baltimore. And subsequently he brought the spiritual and intellectual experiences of his Anglo-Catholic years as an Episcopal priest into his Roman Catholic ministry, first as a professor at St. Thomas Seminary in Bloomfield, Connecticut, for nine years and then as pastor of St. Francis of Assisi parish in South Windsor, Connecticut, from 1963 until his retirement in 1971.

At his funeral liturgy in 1987, celebrated in Litchfield, Connecticut, by Bishop Peter Rosazza, a student of Gordon's at St. Thomas Seminary, Paul Moore, the retired Episcopal bishop of New York, and as a young man a protégé of Gordon's, offered the eulogy. Bishop Moore remembered that, as he put it, "Gordon was not completely happy on either side of the Tiber" (north for Anglican England, south for Catholic Rome). And recently, these many years later, Father Barry Swain, present-day rector of the Church of the Resurrection, recalled that when he chauffeured to Connecticut Father Edgar Wells, Bishop James Montgomery, and Father Leslie Lang in order to visit Gordon in a nursing home during his final illness (his activities had been curtailed by a stroke ten years earlier), the three of them had to wait because he was visibly counseling someone in his room. Then, in that last conversation they asked him if he would make the move to Rome if he had it to do it all over again. Readers will have to ponder these columns to guess the answer.[4]

"The Way of Christ," Gordon's weekly column in the Hartford *Catholic Transcript* from 1960 to 1969, is a record of his vision of Christianity; the supremely appropriate title of the column is the earliest label of the Christian community, followers of "the way" (Acts 9:2; 19:9 and 23; 22:4; 24:14 and 22). To make the case that Gordon's vision invites comparison with Newman's, I trace the trajectory of Newman's accomplishments in England and influence in America up to and including Gordon's seminary formation, and then present the columns. They were not a commentary on Newman but were inspired and brought into focus by Newman's life and experience, which for Gordon provided the light along the *way*.[5] And

4. For helpful historical and anecdotal data here, I thank Father Swain, and both Bishop Peter Rosazza and Father Lawrence Bock of the Catholic Archdiocese of Hartford.

5. In a 1962 column, "Meeting an Old Friend," he describes his response to the advice

whereas the tracts and "parochial and plain sermons" were long, complex of ideas, and (in the case of the tracts) abstract, the "Way of Christ" columns were short, concrete, and presented a single idea. Gordon's personal journey—can we call it an odyssey?—paralleled Newman's personal journey, well summed up, it seems to me, in the title of the present book, *An Anglo-Catholic Visionary for Modern America: Gordon Butler Wadhams and "The Way of Christ."*

In 1833, Newman and his fellow churchmen, John Keble and William Hurrell Froude, joined then by Edward Pusey, agreed to the formation of a movement to promote apostolic succession and reforms of doctrine and discipline in the Anglican Church. High profile churchmen in previous centuries, such as Archbishop William Laud during the reign of Charles I, had strongly promoted apostolic tradition, but the Tractarians and their *Tracts of the Times* represented the first concerted efforts to do so. By July 1835, sixty-five tracts had been published. Tract XC, Newman's epoch-making essay on the Anglican confession known as the Thirty-Nine Articles, was published January 27, 1841. Owen Chadwick lists a number of "Protestant" observations in the tract, such as "we are greatly offended at the received Roman view of transubstantiation" to give the lie to accusation that Newman made it "possible for English clergy to believe all the doctrines of the Roman Catholic Church." But he adds, "the battle over Tract XC ended Newman's usefulness to the Church of England."[6]

Yet, this effort was not so concerted at the beginning. The suppression of ten Church of Ireland bishoprics as part of an arrangement with Roman Catholic authorities moved John Keble, Anglican priest and professor of poetry at Oxford, to condemn the action in a sermon that quickly achieved notoriety. Under the influence of Keble, William Hurrell Froude, Anglican priest and university tutor, briefly marked the movement. With Newman, he drafted a declaration attacking government interference in church affairs, and as they worked together he became a beloved friend and religious inspiration to Newman. After he died in 1836 at age thirty-two, Newman mourned the loss for years. Edward Pusey made contact as an Oxford fellow with Newman and the others in 1823, but then was off to Germany to study Hebrew and theology for two years. Upon his return he was ordained

to spend a lifetime studying an admired personality. He wrote," I . . . made my choice, John Henry Newman," and explained how knowledge was here a deep relationship. For the full column, see pp. 24–25 below. The definitive biography of Newman is Ker, *John Henry Newman.*

6. Chadwick, *Victorian Church*, vol. 1: 183, 188.

a priest and then appointed Regius professor of Hebrew at Oxford. Working with the other Tractarians, he published essays on fasting and baptism. After Newman's departure, he was the most respected voice for Anglo-Catholicism, especially remembered for his sermons on auricular confession and the presence of Christ in the Eucharist. In an 1851 letter, Pusey offered a dramatic definition of the whole movement. "Tractarianism, as it is called, or, as I believe it to be, the Catholic Faith, will survive in the Church of England while the Scriptures are reverenced, and the Ecumenical Councils received, and the Creeds recited, and the Episcopal Succession continues, and union with Christ her Head is cherished, and she acquiesce not, God forbid! in the denial of any article of the Faith."[7]

For Newman, the university church of St. Mary the Virgin and his residence at Littlemore, near Oxford, were both a joy and a sorrow in his turning-point years—especially in his last months there. An unparalleled success as a preacher, he felt the heavy pressure of appearing to be an Anglican divine as he made his way through discomfort, dissatisfaction, and the partial rejection of Anglicanism in the years leading up to 1841. He then accepted responsibility of the parish church of St. Mary in Littlemore and converted an old coach staging post into a larger building for himself and for a small group attracted to a community life of prayer and asceticism. The joy and trials of community life became, at the end, the pain of separation, when Newman left Littlemore and his responsibilities for the church and community for the Church of Rome.

As Newman and like-minded colleagues were publishing *The Tracts of the Times*, similar theological viewpoints and ritual goals developed in the United States.[8] John Henry Hobart, bishop of New York from 1816 to 1830, ensured the foundation of General Theological Seminary in New City as the Episcopal counterpart to a Catholic major seminary. Anglo-Catholicism at General Theological Seminary developed parallel to, and sometimes in relation to, the Oxford Movement. Powel Dawley writes,

7. Quoted in Cameron, "John Henry Newman," in Smart, *Nineteenth Century Religious Thought*, vol. 2, 77.

8. The Episcopal Church in America was Anglo-Catholic before the fact, in that the first post-Revolution bishop in America, Samuel Seabury, was consecrated in Scotland on November 14, 1784. Daniel Handschy writes, "Seabury undertook to introduce the Eucharistic liturgy of the Scottish Episcopal Church into his church in Connecticut and into the rest of the American Church. The Scottish Church, in its disestablished and persecuted state, had recovered the sense of the Eucharistic sacrifice as central to the worship of the Church." See Brown, *Oxford Handbook*, 472.

"At first the *Tracts* created little stir among Episcopalians in this country, largely because of their emphasis upon a high doctrine of the Church and its sacraments, the necessity of apostolic succession, the appeal to the ancient Church Fathers and the authority of tradition had long been familiar principles to old-fashioned high Churchmen. There was thought to be little in them that Bishop Seabury [first Episcopal bishop in America] had not bequeathed to Connecticut churchmen, or that Bishop Hobart had not maintained throughout his ministry. Bishop Onderdonk [fourth bishop of New York], for example, praised the doctrine of the *Tracts* as 'being the same with that which he has taught for many years, even long before the movement in Great Britain.'"[9]

Newman's live sermons, which fascinated his young hearers at Oxford, moved the General Theological seminarians who read them stateside to promotion of Tractarian theology and spirituality. Reactions from Episcopal evangelicals among the clergy and seminary students were, however, more negative than were the anti-Tractarian reactions in England. Wild rumors circulated, everything from accusations that some seminarians advocated the complete acceptance of all things Roman to the belief that there were Jesuits in disguise among them! In fact, there were few conversions to Rome, and four of the most involved seminarians, expelled at the time, were later ordained Episcopal priests; none of them subsequently departed for Rome. Stormy times these were for General Theological, though, starting in the mid-nineteenth century with declining enrollment, neglect or rejection of the institution by a coterie of American bishops, and tensions between evangelical deans and ritualist students. The solution was the deanship of Eugene Hoffman, from 1879 to 1902. Hoffman was educated, cultivated, wealthy, and dedicated to making "General Theological Seminary a place where men could receive the finest preparation that could be provided for the priesthood of the Church." Physically this entailed the planning and construction of the new quadrangles and the High Church Chapel of the Good Shepherd, with a tower inspired by Magdalen tower at Oxford. Spiritually this entailed promoting community life and reforming the curriculum, a process brought to conclusion under Hoffman's successor, and the setting for the seminary years of Gordon Wadhams.[10]

But what can an "Anglo-Catholic vision" possibly be when the most complete history of Anglo-Catholicism in recent decades is subtitled "A

9. Dawley, *General Theological Seminary*, 147.

10. Dawley, *General Theological Seminary*, 145, 249.

Study in Ambiguity"?[11] Certainly there were different forms of Anglo-Catholicism in England and America and they enjoyed—or suffered—different fortunes. The idea of Gordon Allport, the mid-twentieth-century psychologist, that "there are as many types of religious experience as there are religiously inclined mortals upon the earth"[12] is worth adapting to the Anglo-Catholic experience: there are as many types of Anglo-Catholic experience as there are Catholic-identifying Anglicans. But we can try to describe the commonalities and the variations of these Anglo-Catholicisms (perhaps best to use the plural). They have transformed the Anglican Church—in the US, the Episcopal Church—such that their very success has led to a sidelined existence, but even this sidelined existence is a guarantee that the ideas and goals of Anglo-Catholicism will be regularly reviewed and reposted within orthodox Anglicanism.[13]

Historians of Anglo-Catholicism of past decades have been wary of any single all-encompassing definition, relying instead on broad description.[14] W.S.F. Pickering maintained that the Anglo-Catholicisms had a daughter-to-mother relationship with the more serene and balanced Oxford Movement of the Newman era. In the period before World War I, flamboyantly Catholicized clergy finished as converts to Rome or as holdouts in the Anglican parish circuit. Nevertheless, the dedication of many of these priests to the poor in city parishes and their engagement as chaplains in the war won general admiration in England, virtually eliminating the antagonism of earlier decades. After the war, a series of congresses were organized to coordinate and enhance the Anglo-Catholic mission—in 1920, 1927, 1930, and 1933. Large venues were required: Royal Albert Hall, St. Paul's Cathedral, and White City Stadium. Ceremonies were grandiose and lecturers were eloquent, no one more than the missionary bishop of Zanzibar, Frank Weston, who proclaimed, "We now stand for the Catholic Faith common to the East and West. We are not concerned with the shibboleths of low, Church, high Church, broad Church, liberal, modernist, or even the new 'non-party' party. We stand or fall with Christ's Church, Catholic

11. Pickering, *Anglo-Catholicism*.

12. Allport, *Individual and His Religion*, 30.

13. See the brief discussion of Nashotah House below.

14. Even so, Peter Nockles divides the theory-based histories of the Oxford Movement into three categories: those who see the Movement as (1) an instrument of providence, (2) the means of bringing Newman and some others into the Roman Church, or (3) the subversion of the rightfully Protestant essence of the Anglican Church. See Brown, *Oxford Handbook*, 605.

and apostolic. And we wait patiently till the Holy Father and the orthodox Patriarchs recognize us as of their own stock. We are not a party: we are those in the Anglican Communion who refuse to be limited by party rules and party creeds. Our appeal is to the Catholic Creed, to Catholic worship, and to Catholic practice."[15] Although disagreements persisted about some Marian devotions and some ceremonies involving the consecrated Eucharistic breads (e.g., benediction of the blessed sacrament), the number of enrolled participants went from 13,000 in 1920 to 70,000 in 1933. By that time Anglo-Catholic obligations were listed as Mass on Sunday, communion three times a year, confession once a year, fasting on Friday, almsgiving, and obedience to church marriage laws.[16]

For reforming spiritual life, the new religious orders of priests and nuns took their inspiration from Catholic models, the Vincentians in particular, but also the Franciscans. The largest Anglican Benedictine monastic community at Nashdom was established 1914. Orders of nuns were founded earliest of all (in Newman's day!), beginning with the Sisterhood of the Holy Cross and the Community of St. Mary the Virgin. And for reforming social and political life, the experience of slum conditions pushed Anglo-Catholic priests to embrace revolution and even Marxist solutions to the problems of the twentieth century. The majority of English bishops were cool towards, if not wary of, the Anglo-Catholicisms, thus presenting a dilemma to Anglo-Catholic priests who affirmed the necessity of hierarchy. On one hand, it was impossible to reject the orders of a bishop; on the other hand, impossible to accept his watering down of Catholicism.[17] But the late-twentieth century archbishops of Canterbury were moderately to completely committed to Anglo-Catholicism. Pickering writes, "Michael Ramsey, Archbishop of Canterbury from 1961 to 1974 was the most Anglo-Catholic primate there had ever been."[18] The rapprochement to Roman Catholicism naturally combined with a rapprochement to Eastern Orthodoxy and brought a new focus to Anglican ecumenism. Ecumenical fervor characterized the Malines (Belgium) conversations presided over by Cardinal Désiré Mercier between 1921 and 1925, although considerable anxiety developed on the Anglican side in the years that followed. Pursuit, then, of the relationship with the Eastern Orthodox (e.g., the Russian

---

15. *Oxford Handbook*, 180–81.

16. Pickering, *Anglo-Catholicism*, 180–81, 56, 60.

17. Pickering, *Anglo-Catholicism*, 154.

18. Pickering, *Anglo-Catholicism*, 152.

Orthodox Church) and the Oriental Orthodox (e.g., the Egyptian Coptic Church), which was less threatening to both Anglicans and Orthodox than any moves toward reunion with Rome.[19] These preoccupations were not central for the priests, parishes, and small idiosyncratic religious communities called the "outer fringes of the Church of England" by Michael Yelton in his positive-in-the-main study, *Anglo Papalism: An Illustrated History, 1900–1960*. But their actual preoccupations with the details of Roman Catholic ritual lost all practical significance following the liturgical reforms of the Second Vatican Council, which de-emphasized or did away with some of the accretions that they cherished the most. By way of exception, the book of Nashdom Abbey's Dom Gregory Dix, *The Shape of the Liturgy*, published in 1945, influenced scholars and the cultivated reading public in both the Anglican and Roman Catholic Churches, and was certainly well known to the theologians reforming the Mass and sacraments at the Vatican Council. Dix was a good friend of Gordon Wadhams, touring New York churches and liturgies with him and supporting Gordon's early commitment to Roman Catholicism.[20]

In twentieth century America, Episcopal churchmen have lucidly sorted out the historical highlights and random features of Anglo-Catholicism. Between the two world wars, Walter Herbert Stowe, rector of Christ Church, New Brunswick, New Jersey, focused in a long essay on the Tractarian tradition as it was realized in England and the United States. And after World War II, George E. DeMille, a priest of the Episcopal diocese of Albany, NY, published the book-length history, *The Catholic Movement in the American Episcopal Church*, showing how these key qualities developed in the nineteenth and twentieth centuries.

The Oxford Movement, writes Stowe, sought to re-establish the identity between the Anglican Church of the nineteenth century and the pre-Reformation English church, emphasizing the seven sacraments and apostolic succession. The key point, however, is that "Christ is the end; the [basic elements]—Creeds, Bible, Ministry, and Sacraments—are the means." Creeds and bible are creations of the church guided by the Holy Spirit, so valid church tradition is crucial to the correct interpretation of scripture. Stowe writes that "in the field of biblical criticism Anglo-Catholicism may be classed as cautious without being reactionary, in contrast to both Roman Catholicism and Protestant Fundamentalism." He values

19. Rowell, *Vision Glorious*, 204–17.

20. Yelton, *Anglo Papalism*, chapter six. Dix, *Shape of the Liturgy*.

the truth claims of ecumenical—and local—councils insofar as they gain church-wide acceptance; he values private interpretation, also, insofar as it can be theologically confirmed. The ministry of bishops and priests is also essential to the life of the church, but Stowe cites the existing historical evidence that these ministries varied in form and expression from place to place and from century to century. Here, he relies on J. G. Lightfoot, who wrote that "the episcopate was formed, not out of the Apostolic order by localization, but out of the presbyteral by elevation."[21]

Stowe's solid presentation of the Oxford Movement contained very few historical inaccuracies, but among them were the notions that the primacy of the bishop of Rome had no factual basis at all in early church polity, and that the Eastern Orthodox and Greek Catholics (!) never submitted to Rome. These certainly had little bearing on his overall study, which he justifiably concluded on a high note of faith and optimism. "When all is said and done, Anglo-Catholicism is a vigorous, virile movement which had profoundly affected the Anglican Communion. It was never so strong as it is today. It is definite in faith and practice, yet flexible in secondary matters. It has unbroken continuity with the Holy Catholic Church of the past, yet is awake to modern needs. It has respect for authority and love for liberty. Provincial in origin, it has attained a world-wide outlook and status."[22]

DeMille provided further details. Contemporary to the Anglo-Catholic congresses in England were the Catholic congresses of 1925 in New Haven and 1933 in Philadelphia—where Father Julian Hamlin linked experiences of the sacraments with promotion and nourishing of the human spirit in the machine age.[23] At the center of official Episcopal Church action, of course, was the revision of the prayer book that came to fruition in 1928. Psalms were provided for every Sunday of the year, biblical texts—sometimes corrected—now included the apocrypha, with their selection and use reflecting traditions of the church fathers. The Eucharist was reformed by placing the Lord's Prayer at the end of the canon and the Prayer of Humble Access just before the priest's communion. There was provision for a requiem Eucharist, a nuptial Eucharist, and commemoration of the saints.[24]

Before and after Stowe and DeMille, the main features of Anglo-Catholicism were lived out and promoted by the eminently respected community

21. Stowe, *Anglo-Catholicism*, 7, 19.
22. Stowe, *Anglo-Catholicism*, 2, 3, 19.
23. DeMille, *Catholic Movement*, 203.
24. DeMille, *Catholic Movement*, 200.

of Nashotah House, the Episcopal theological seminary in Nashotah, Wisconsin. Founded in 1842 specifically to propagate the Anglo-Catholicism of the Oxford Movement, Nashotah House relied in the beginning on support from the Bishop Saint Tikhon of Alaska, later Moscow Patriarch of the Russian Orthodox Church. This foundational ecumenical feature of Nashotah House issued in twentieth-century liaisons with St. Vladimir's Orthodox Seminary in New York, Sacred Heart Catholic Seminary in Wisconsin; and in mid-century the Polish National Catholic Church sent some of its seminarians there. Nashotah House with its challenges and successes is a clear reminder that the ways of worship dear to Anglo-Catholic clergy and people, formalized in the 1928 prayer book, were worthwhile in their own right. The former Episcopal bishop of Quincy, Illinois, Keith Ackerman (1994–2008), proposed it as the home base of Anglo-Catholicism in the Episcopal Church.[25] It may be true that the old Anglo-Catholic preoccupations lost all practical significance with the absorption of Anglo-Catholicism into the Episcopal Church, and that the remaining splinter groups, mostly small, have dwindled away into isolation, but the gains made need to be maintained to guarantee their ultimate success.[26]

Gordon's vision was not any one of the varieties of Anglo-Catholicism that figure in the specialized histories, nor a lowest common denominator of the Anglo-Catholicisms, but was an original contribution gradually constructed by news, views, and wise counsels across the more than five hundred columns of "The Way of Christ." I have selected seventy-five and distributed them across five themes:

1. Personal Odyssey.

2. The Great Church and Ecumenism.

3. Liturgy: Tradition and Acculturation.

4. The Bible for Everyone.

5. Spiritual Life and Christian Mission.

Readers will find that I have placed the columns within each section in logical, and not chronological, order. Although Gordon's ideas evolved over the decades, as he himself occasionally notes, the changes are not the central story. Rather, the high drama in his columns results from his year-to-year face-offs with world politics, major church reform, and national trauma.

25. Ackerman, "Anglo-Catholicism."
26. Colin Podmore lists the active small groups in Brown, *Oxford Handbook*, 625–32.

Think the Vietnam war, the Second Vatican Council, and the assassination of President Kennedy! His columns are as alive and pertinent today, as when they were written. True it is, though, that some terminology and style features are time-bound: he always uses the mainline pronouns, instead of recasting sentences in the plural to facilitate the gender-neutral "they," and uses the noun and adjective "negro" instead of "black" or "people of color." I note this up front, so it will not discomfort readers.

It was once said of St. John Henry Newman that he was "all the better a Catholic for having been an Anglican; and, indeed, in a very real sense, he did not cease to be an Anglican when he became a Roman Catholic,"[27] a great line that perfectly describes the life and ministry of Father Gordon Butler Wadhams.

Rector of the Church of the Resurrection, New York City, 1935–1949

27. Fairbairn, *Catholicism*, 79, quoted in Pickering, *Anglo-Catholicism*, 217.

2

Personal Odyssey

GORDON'S FAMILY SHAPED HIS personality and his Christianity, a story he told in some of his most moving columns. His father, his mother, and his grandparents were the foundation of his faith and his vocation. And he dedicated his first column to his grandparents' beloved Catholic housekeeper, whose rustic country church was his first Catholic contact. We look at them through his eyes and we see the goodness and honesty that he made his own. His father, the country doctor who ministered to all his suffering patients, refusing no one and disappearing in winter weather for days at a time from their hometown, Goshen, his mother not sure if he would find his way back. Even though Anglo-Canadian, Gordon's mother could not hold out in that setting and made her country doctor husband set up a practice in Westhampton, on the Atlantic coast of Long Island. Not that she feared the Connecticut winters for herself, because on one wintry eve, she appeared at the baptistery of the Episcopal church in nearby Torrington, Connecticut, to have Gordon baptized, a brave moment remembered years later by the church pastor. She introduced him as a ten-year-old to the Anglo-Canada where she was born, and where he, even then, observed Catholic Franco-Canada with great admiration.

On Long Island, still a boy, Gordon was fascinated by the city churches he saw while on his regular trips to the orthodontist in Manhattan. As the years passed, his father gave himself to his patients with unflagging dedication, never refusing a patient, however indigent or far away from town.

Then, at a moment of great fatigue in his mid-fifties, Dr. Wadhams noti-fied his local hospital, stopped at the Catholic church—he who was not a churchgoer—and twenty minutes later continued on to the hospital, dying under anesthesia although he had assured his wife that this was a minor af-fair. Gordon always rejoiced in the thought that those twenty minutes were spent in the anteroom to heaven.

The life of the convert priest was marked by both high joy and deep sorrow, and Gordon dedicated columns to both sides of the story: home-coming and homesickness. If his fundamental inspiration was Cardinal Newman, the inspiration of his early ministry was the brilliant Father Ron-ald Knox. He described key moments of his years at General Theological Seminary in New York city, as he developed into the Anglo-Catholic priest ordained for the Episcopal Church in 1933, but the years of study at Phil-lips Andover and Yale University, the two years in France, and the year as a teacher at Manlius Academy receive little coverage in the columns and are not included here. Clearly they gave him a superior general education and the capacity for the personalized, elegant English we see in those columns.

As Gordon began his odyssey to Rome, his guides along the way were the priest luminaries of American Catholicism, the scholar-pastors Hans Reinhold and Martin Hellriegel, and the innovative abbot Damasus Winzen, whose monastery of Mount Saviour in Pine City, New York was a model for the broader Christian community. It left Gordon thinking that, were he much younger, he would have chosen "the Benedict option" (as it has been called today).

The Price is Above Rubies—January 7, 1960

In a small graveyard behind one of our earliest mission churches there lie 4 or 5 of the faithful, Pioneer Catholics in a once remote corner of Connecti-cut. Among these humble graves is that of a woman to whom the writer as he reflects, owes much, perhaps everything he has.

In my childhood this woman was the "hired help" at my grand-mother's. We grandchildren spent our summers there. We were carefully brought up to use no familiarity with Mrs. M. . . . . for so were we taught to address her. She was not a servant, for she had come there to "help" my grandmother between whom and herself there was a deep affection. She worked hard and it was somehow conveyed to us that life had not used her kindly. Compassion for her? Yes, but not the least condescension. We loved her and our love was bountifully returned.

There are those today who have not forgotten, nor have ever since tasted the like of her apple pies. In the kitchen and in the society of persons she was an artist. I think, now that I look back on those days, that she was a saint.

That she was different I knew by some intuitive sense. The difference, I knew also, had to do with God. Not that she said anything, for my grandmother would not have wished her to. But different she was.

It was Mrs. M. . . . who gave me my first sight of a Catholic church. One day we went for a walk, she and I. Up the street, past our white-pillared church where my grandfather was senior deacon, on to the then shabbier "north end" we went. We came to the Catholic church. We open the rickety gate in the sadly unsteady fence and walked through grass waist-high to the door. She had the keys—I now realize that she was its custodian during the weeks, sometimes months, between the visits of a priest—and we went inside.

Smells, like sights, linger in one's memory and I can still smell the poverty and meanness of that House. But neither have I forgotten the fascination for me of that holy place. *He* was not there in His special Presence, there being then no resident priest to take care of Him (I did not know that, of course), but His Mother was, and so His foster father. I read with a child's eyes, for the first time, His story along the walls. Only God knows how deep the impression went.

"Work such as hers," wrote the Wise King, "claims its reward; let her life be spoken of with praise at the city gates." Gladly to toil, to bear one's sorrows in secret, to love and beget love in others, to bake a superlative apple pie, and to plant the seed of conversion in the heart of a little boy: what view, think you, does God take of all this?

Ye Snows, Bless the Lord—February 22, 1962

Trapped by a measured 16 inches of snow in my driveway this morning, there is nothing to do while waiting for my good neighbor to finish ploughing his own barnyard before coming to me but to sit here at the window and marvel at the sheer magic of what I see. At hand are my breviary and a copy of Whittier's "Snowbound."

Matins and Lauds, especially Lauds, give me this morning, as a growing light still grey but welcome none the less discloses the winter's wonderland in this the first big snowfall of the year, a fresh sense of the wonderful works of God. And Whittier—"marvellous shapes strange domes and towers"—calls up memories of tales my mother told me of winters in Goshen the first eight years of this century. The benison of cool green summers was more than paid for by the fury of the bad and dreaded months.

My father practiced medicine in Goshen—which in those days, incredible as it seems now, meant the Cornwalls and even Falls Village. Many a winter's afternoon he would harness his horse to the cutter and start for some remote farmhouse. He could well have anticipated Robert Frost's poignant line, "And miles to go before I sleep." (I am sure he must have thought it.) In the meantime, the sun sinking "from sight before it set," with the hour of dusk the snows would come. Once he did not come back for three days until, from farm to farm and finally, to the "center," teams of oxen could open the road. The lines were down and there was no telephone to let my mother know where he was or what had happened. Even a Canadian girlhood had not prepared her for this sort of anxiety. Or, not infrequently, my father would be overturned in a giant snowdrift. That meant freeing the horse to return home by herself—which she would do, sans sleigh, sans passenger.

Eight such winters and my mother, as the saying goes, had "had" it. She persuaded my father to take a practice on Long Island, fearing nevertheless that he would not be happy away from the hills of home. But he was. For a whole kingdom he would not have traded the dunelands and waterways of his beloved and temperate South Shore. Kitty, the horse, went with us and lived out her days well-fed and stout of girth, with nothing to do but receive the affection of those who owed her so much.

I cannot here resist telling of my father's first automobile, a Cadillac boasting one cylinder and irreverently called a "one-lunger." On our first trip back to Goshen, the car gave out half way between Torrington and Goshen—on "watering-trough hill," to those who know the place. To our embarrassment and my grandfather's delight, it had to be towed up the hill by a team of oxen. For years thereafter my father judged the worth of his cars by their ability, or, more often, their failure to make this hill. It was a long day indeed before he had one that could "take it in high."

This morning I got out a letter written to us in my grandfather's beautiful hand. It describes what he could see beyond a two-feet snowdrift outside the dining-room window. Tireless fisherman that he was, he told no "fish-stories." A deacon in the Congregational Church, he had a reputation for telling the sober truth. His letter bears the date May 17, 1917.

Grace is Added Upon Grace—April 21, 1960

On the 29th of March I took note of the death in his one hundred second year of the Reverend Dr. J. Chauncey Linsley, rector emeritus of Trinity Episcopal Church, Torrington. It may interest you to know what manner of man he was.

In 1904 my mother, a Canadian-born Anglican, braved the disapproval of my father's parents and had me baptized in Trinity Church by Dr. Linsley. My Congregationalist grandparents and great-aunts did not attend, for in their view I was simply being taken through "the back door to Rome." (Little they knew!) It must have been a forlorn occasion for my mother and god-parents, for they were alone that day. I have always cherished my mother's courage in standing fast by her convictions. Four years later we moved to Long Island and thus lost touch with our rector.

In 1930 I entered the General Theological Seminary in New York. Alumni Day was observed during the Michaelmas term. That day there was a knock at my door. I opened it and there stood a magnificent old gentleman who introduced himself as Dr. Linsley. "Are you," he asked, "the same 'Wadhams Gordon Butler' whom I baptized in Torrington? I read your name on the class lists and it stirred memories of a mother bringing her child to me on stormy winter's day for Baptism."

This remarkable interest in souls remained keen and active, I am told by Dr. Linsley's friends, up to the end. Not content at retirement in 1927 to sit and fold his hands—he had served his parish in Torrington for more than a generation—Dr. Linsley went to Berkeley Divinity School to occupy the chair of Pastoral Theology where for another twenty-four years he put his experience at the disposal of admiring and grateful students.

I mentioned my dear mother's courage and loyalty to convictions. When the time came to put my hand to the plough, you may well imagine that I thought of all this: of Dr. Linsley, of the hosts of persons and influences that had, under God, given me so much. I had known many men like Dr. Linsley, nor do I forget them today; men who taught me to pray, men who gave me a love of the Bible, men whose lives were priest-like and wholly disinterested, men who had a love of souls, men who tried to give me the mind of Christ. It was, you may well believe, hard to take a step which appeared to spurn all of this.

I could never have done it had I not at the time the conviction that what I was about to do, far from denying, was in reality fulfilling the past. We converts do not give up whatever is good and true and enduring in our background. We add to it, and what is added only heightens the grace and glory of all God gave us in the beginning. Grace upon grace.

Another Stage on the Road—June 23, 1960

Re-reading with my juniors this spring a profoundly Christian novel stirred memories of my boyhood and of a singular grace then vouchsafed to me. Louis Hémon's "Maria Chapdelaine," now available in translation in paper covers, is set in the Province of Quebec soon after the turn of our century. It tells of the hard life of the "habitant," his life-long battle with the forest, the winter, the perilously short growing season. Childlike faith, a genius for sacrifice, humble submission to God's daily, always mysterious, Providence; these are the stuff of the peasant's character. One cannot, I think, have read this book without being the better and stronger for it.

I was ten years old when my mother took me to visit the land of her birth. By that time, I had absorbed, through the multiplicity of influence that affect a child's mind, the notion that the English civilization in Canada was superior to the French; that the "Canuck" belonged to a subject people, ignorant, inferior and, of course, "priest-ridden." This I took on simple authority.

Our hotel in Montreal was opposite the Cathedral. From our windows the first morning I saw a sight altogether foreign to me; Capuchin friars walking sandal-shod in the streets, sisters by the score, priests wearing the soutane. Was it contrariness that made the sight attractive to me? My mother did not share my enthusiasm.

Some days later in the train to Quebec I saw the logjams at Trois-Rivières and the nimble lumberjacks, the "habitant" farms, boys and girls in the charge of priests and brothers outside their schools, wayside shrines with Cross and instruments of the Passion, gleaming spire-topped churches sheltering ("as a hen gathers her chickens under her wings") the neat houses clustered round about. A Catholic way of life is what I saw and even then in all my ignorance I somehow sensed that it was good. With a child's directness I concluded that what mattered most here was religion. Could it be this that made my mother's people look down their noses? I could find no other reason.

It was years later that I could begin to see this in its true light. Willa Cather's "Shadows on the Rock" and Henry Beston's "The St. Lawrence" started me on my independent exploration of French Canada. Then I discovered "Maria Chapdelaine." Motor trips summer after summer strengthened the impression made by these books. By this time I knew France and, ironically, I found French Canada more French, if possible, certainly more Catholic, than the France I had come to know and love.

It is a privilege these latter years to have in one's classes young men who are descended from the founders of New France. They have the toughness and the resilience of their forebears. They do honor to the faith and the piety that are their inheritance. I am happy to pay this small tribute to them.

Another Boyhood Memory—January 31, 1963

There is not one of us who cannot point to a time in life when God shed his grace in strange ways and in singular abundance. For me these times are so numerous that I would find it hard to list them all. But of these one seems in retrospect so strange that the memory is as vivid as was the actuality.

I could not have been more than eleven or twelve at the time it was decided by my parents that something had to be done about (of all things) straightening my teeth. Orthodontists were rare in those days and the one chosen for me lived in Brooklyn in the winter, summering near us on the South Shore from June to September. The work began during the summer. I do not know what boys and girls go through nowadays—their braces look innocent enough, but in my day wearing them was a school in martyrdom. At one point in this seemingly unending torment I had in my mouth an engine alongside which the wheel and rack would look like toys: one contrivance of platinum wire upstairs, which only the surgeon could remove, one down, and the two connected by extremely tight rubber bands.

When September came, I had to follow the dentist to his lair in Brooklyn. On two Saturdays my mother came with me. Thereafter I made the trip alone, taking the Long Island at half-past seven, changing in Jamaica for the Brooklyn local, getting off at Nostrand Avenue and walking the three or four blocks to Dr. Keppies's house. There, week after week, I suffered the turn of the screw, literally, of this odious machine. This had its compensations, albeit short lived, for I was the only one in my village to wear braces, and I could exhibit them on request, and the only one my age who could go to New York by himself, and this I could boast of. Anyway, each Saturday, I was on my own from eleven to four. I learned how to get by subway to New York and thence to Penn Station for the train home.

How did I spend my time? So completely off-beat is this you will find it hard to credit. I visited Catholic churches. To account for this (in a boy of twelve), abnormal interest I am at a loss; what first aroused it I do not know; but there isn't a church between 30th and 42nd Streets, east or west, that I haven't known these almost fifty years. Saint John's, the Capuchin church, and Saint Francis of Assisi, the Franciscan shrine, near Penn Station were my favorite haunts and to this day I love them both. They are in a sense home to me.

The mass at noonday was especially exciting, deliciously bewildering to a boy who hadn't the slightest notion of what was happening. I couldn't find out, for I had no one to ask. But I watched the chances of vestments from green to violet, to white and back to green, then again to violet, then white, and back to green. Why this curious kaleidoscope, thought I, only heaven knew and these hordes of people whose behavior I tried to copy—genuflections, crossings, beating of breast, and bowing. I saw the crib at Christmas and the odd veiling of the images at Passiontide. I thought how wonderful to have been born one of these Catholics, for surely this kind of religion was far more entertaining than anything I knew at home. I dared to imagine the day when, grown up, I might—perish the thought of what my parents would say—assert myself and be a Catholic. Oh, yes, the tingling fear that I might one day be discovered for the imposter I was, that someone in these churches would learn that I had no business there. I dreaded the moment when a priest would find me out and hustle me out the door. Had I known anything about the ancient practice of dismissing the catechumens, of banishing the notorious sinner, or of excluding the heretic from these mysteries, I should have understood perfectly, so much the outsider did I feel. Back home at night I would be asked by my mother, "What did you do today?" "Oh, . . . things." "Well, what things?" "Just . . . things," was my evasive boy-like answer. Wise woman that she was, she didn't pin me down.

That on the Good Ground—March 16, 1961

The Parable of the Sower reminds me without fail of my dear father. He was a "beloved physician," the old-fashioned country doctor. More than that, he was the finest man I have ever known.

The gentlest, most tolerant of men, he was never known to say aught against anyone. If he had cause for disapproval, his silence was rebuke enough. Only once can I remember falling under his spoken wrath. The occasion was my refusal (he was a witness to it from the steps of his office) to let a Negro sit with me in the front seat as I drove him home after my father had treated him for an injury. I have never forgotten how small my father made me feel.

My father could not say No to any appeal to his skill. He worked day, and night. For the last three years of his life, he took no holiday. He died, altogether used up, at fifty-two. A dozen men today cover his territory which, allowing for increases in population, gives one some idea of his practice in the villages that line the south shore of Long Island's Suffolk County.

Of his religion? It is hard to write of this. I think that my father was a rebel from the cold and rigid Puritanism that was his heritage from New England. He did not attend church although he contributed to all the churches in the village. He knew little of "organized" religion, and the little he knew he didn't like. The parish priest of our village and many nuns from neighboring towns, whom my father had cared for, came to the house to pay their respects; all the local clergy were present at his funeral. No man, it seems to me, could have better lived the Sermon on the Mount than did my father; and yet, I cannot say that he was a religious man.

The morning he died, after delivering a baby in the Negro quarter of the village, his chauffeur drove him to Southampton where he was to undergo surgery. How really ill he was he knew, but this he kept from my mother and me. The surgery was to be "minor" and we were to visit him in mid-morning. This was as he wanted it.

On the way over they went through the village of Good Ground. (Isn't that a charming name? It has since been stupidly changed to Hampton Bays.) It was about seven o'clock. As they approached St. Rose's Catholic church, my father ordered the car stopped. People were going into church for Mass. My father got out and went into the church. He stayed perhaps twenty minutes. We do not know what happened during that visit, for my father died within the hour, under anesthesia before ever the knife was used.

Members of my family, some of them, did not credit this story, regarding it as the apocryphal invention of a well-meaning but distraught servant. But I did, and do. I cannot account for its being made up. And when I read the Parable of the Sower, I take comfort in reflecting that "that on the good ground are they who, with a good and pure hear, bring forth fruit with patience."

When Exile is Homecoming—August 24, 1961

In the hearing of many of you (perhaps of too many to justify making this the subject of an essay) I have used this paradox to describe the two-fold experience of the convert. For conversion brings with it an acute sense of exile. One is cut off from the past and for a time this sense of being a stranger is painful indeed. Like Ruth, one stands "weeping amid the alien corn." Or, as with Abraham, the summons to "get thee out of thy country, and from thy kindred, and out of thy father's house" is terrifying and induces in one's being a profound, nearly heart-breaking nostalgia.

But this is little by little overborne by a singular grace, that is, a sense altogether deep and strengthening of at last belonging. No one can know as does the convert the measure of his peace after so long travail; his certainty after so long groping in the valley of the shadows; his new-found strength; his having at length come home. What was at first a cruel divorce from the familiar is seen now to have been the means of joining himself indissolubly to the imperishable Christ. "The Parting of Friends"—for Newman said it all in this sermon—means now the fullness of the friendship of Christ. The forsaking of one's father's house is now to him an entrance into those mansions made ready in the heavenly Father's kingdom. In a word, one comes home; home to the pillar and ground of truth and life; to Rome, the storehouse of grace; home to the eternal city, outward and earthly sign and foretaste of that other City, the Kin's own, "which hath the everlasting foundations, whose builder and maker is God."

And all this I have often illustrated by recalling what it was like to visit Quebec after my conversion. Often, for years before it, I went to Quebec and there reveled in the power and glory of the Church. Visiting the historic sanctuaries, touched as always by the people's devotion, coming, I think, to appreciate these as keenly as an outsider can, I nevertheless knew that I did not belong. Would I ever? That was the question I could not ask myself and for long years did not, nor dared to entertain.

Imagine, then, what joy there was in my return in 1949. The charming basilica, Monseigneur Laval's tomb, the Convent of the Ursulines—with eager steps these and other holy places were sought out again, this time with a new enthusiasm, that of the pilgrim and sojourner who knows that all these in a sense are his. They belong to him and he belongs! I think that this happiness can for me be exceeded only by seeing Rome, if ever God grants me that benison, but this year again I return to Quebec.

What a pity it is that our Protestant friends cannot somehow realize that coming into the Church is not a giving-up so much as a receiving, not a forsaking so much as an entrance, not so much the rude clanging of the gates behind one as the opening ahead in all its splendor of the very Gate of Heaven itself.

'In Psalms, Hymns, and Songs'—March 10, 1960

A modest but fine little paper coming from Boston and given to the study of the "living parish" recently asked this question: "Are converts to the Catholic Church ever homesick?" The answer is "yes."

If the convert has come from a church having a set form of public worship, as do the Episcopal and Lutheran churches, there are things he will miss, and miss sorely. This is not to say that he will not learn to do without them or that, doing without them, he will be unhappy, for he will have learned that his contentment is due not to the trimmings, but to the essentials of his new-found Faith. Yet he is aware of a gentle irony in that the things he misses, most of them, are Catholic both in origin and content, as is everything that is enduring in his background. One of the most obvious of these is the congregational singing of hymns.

Now we have here no thought of instructing our betters, for unlike the inspired Psalmist, we are not "wiser than our teacher." We think, too, that we know by this time as well as anyone the problems of the overcrowded urban parish; we do not, therefore, urge the overthrow of settled procedures that seem to make the best of the very nearly insoluble problem of accommodating great numbers of persons on a given Sunday morning. Rather, we have in mind the village parish where the tempo is still leisurely (there are a few left), the parish where there are evening services, and above all, the parish where an attempt is made to offer the last Mass with a degree of solemnity and freedom from hurry. Here and at these times a processional and recessional hymn sung by choir and people are altogether possible and desirable.

Singing "psalms and hymns and spiritual songs" has from the beginning in Christian tradition been a spur to the wholehearted praise of God. What hymns have we in mind? They are noble hymns in translations of manifest strength and beauty. They are all of renowned Catholic authorship, full of sound doctrine and devoid of mawkishness. Many of the tunes to which they are set are traditional in the Church, and all are of undoubted musical excellence. Yet to play and to sing them require no unusual or professional skill, although the art of accompanying and singing hymns is learned only through practice and familiarity.

Take the following as examples: for Advent, "O come, o come, Emmanuel;" "Of the Father's love begotten," by Prudentius, for Christmastide; for the Epiphany, also by Prudentius, the exquisite "Earth hath many a noble city"; for Passiontide, "The royal banners forward go" and the famous Passion Chorale, "O sacred Head so wounded"; for Easter Day, "The strife is o'er." It is on these and their like that we were raised and, frankly, after twelve years we are homesick for them still. Will they be sung, some of them, in heaven?

"Homesick?" you say, Yes, the word is carefully chosen. For these hymns are the precious, though neglected, possession of our true home, the Catholic Church. It is this that adds to the pain. We remember hearing a convert-priest tell how, one afternoon, he stood in the great porch of York Minister and heard the choir and people singing one of these hymns. Weeping, he left the church for he could no longer bear the sound.

Meeting an Old Friend—November 22, 1962

Who can afford to invest in current books? For our money nothing pays off nowadays so liberally as biography, for this is the day of able biographers and generally shabby novelists. In this matter the advice of a great teacher has been the rule of my adult years. (I have written of this once before, but it will bear repeating.) "Choose," he said, "one great personage of the past or one period in history or some one subject that strongly appeals to you and determine by systematic reading to know all you can about that person or subject. This will occupy the rest of your lifetime." I took his advice and made my choice, John Henry Newman.

What knowledge does one gain from such a discipline? Not the kind and not enough certainly to sustain a doctoral thesis, for that is not one's object. Admittedly, if mine were a tidier mind and a better memory, I should know about J. H. N. far more than I do: minute facts, dates, events and figures of the times. But there is a different way of knowledge, like the knowledge one has of a friend he loves. It is knowledge gained as only true knowledge of a person can be, that is, through love—I mean deep admiration, full trust, the certainty of never being betrayed nor let down, and the joy of the friend's continuing self-disclosure. Indeed, what is this in our human relationships but the counterpart of our progressive knowledge of God?

Having over the years read the many fine biographies of Newman, I returned to him the other day when the latest to appear was put in my hands by our librarian, Meriol Trevor's *Newman: The Pillar of the Cloud*. It was like meeting an old friend whom one had not seen for a long time. As always the reunion was a happy one. Because the book is a thick one (and another volume is promised) this life allows of sitting down very often in the companionship of one's old friend. And as always, one learns something new and fresh and hitherto unnoticed about him. For instance, his family and his boyhood: it is as though he said, "I've never told you much about my parents, have I? And we were not boys together." Well, to this biographer I owe the knowledge that Newman's parents were not bluestockings who frowned on wining and dancing and play-going; they were not the strait-laced "evangelicals" I had thought them. Their home was gay and bright and full of fun, that is, until the failure of Mr. Newman's bank. And even then they took their reverses in good and courageous part.

And as for John's boyhood, somehow the true story had never for me been quite so sympathetically told, for here in these opening pages he is all boy—extravagantly gifted, to be sure, but a leader liked and looked up to by his peers, at school the prankster and the wit, and hero throughout these years to his brothers and sisters.

It is not long however, before the young Newman, not at Trinity in Oxford, grows up by our poor standards before his time. Here we see him (and a moving sight it is) still in his teens faint from overwork, asleep over his books, taking on hours of tutoring to pay for his brother's schooling, keeping a meticulous journal of his spiritual faults and failings, getting into arguments with his father and charging himself with the burden of the blame, putting "holiness before peace," and learning the hard way of unremitting prayer. In short, here already is the Newman of promise, the man who one day by heroic struggle and generous correspondence to grace will achieve the measure of the fullness of the stature of Christ; Newman, the holy man; Newman, I think, the saint.

A Personal Debt of Thanks—March 24, 1960

I have a special reason for esteeming the biography of Ronald Knox by Evelyn Waugh. I did not have the honor of knowing Monsignor Knox, but I have friends who did. Among my treasures is a letter from him in his own hand in answer to a question that occupied my mind during the years of indecision. As you might expect, his answer was kindly but somewhat blunt. I have wondered since if at the time it made more of an impression that I was able to realize.

Thirty-five years ago, when I was preparing for the Anglican ministry, "Ronnie" Knox was the embodiment of "advanced," that is, pro-Roman, high churchmanship. His name was a watchword to us and his genius our proudest boast.

Those were the days of his devastating satires and his brilliant sermons on reunion with the Holy See. We read them, memorized portions of them, quoted them, and knew that we were in touch with perhaps the keenest mind, certainly the sharpest wit, of our day. Friends returning from England would bring us word of "Ronnie's" latest triumph—usually an incident, or a clever retort, or a piece of apologetic for our cause, bringing dismay to his ecclesiastical superiors, for he was then the despair of the Anglican hierarchy, the "Peck's Bad Boy" of the Church of England. His "going over" was a blow, but we soon adopted other heroes. It was not until the appearance of his *Spiritual Aeneid* and his translation of the Scriptures that we renewed acquaintance with him, only to realize again the greatness of our loss.

Later, many years later, I learned from a near neighbor, a fellow-convert, who as a young man had been at Oxford with Knox, of other facets of his brilliance his genius for improvising limericks to suit an occasion, his uncommon grasp of classical literature, his proverbial devotion to his friends, his distaste for almost everything modern. I did not need Mr. Waugh to tell me all of this.

What Evelyn Waugh has given me (and because of this I have read and re-read his biography) is the moving portrait of a deeply humble man, an essentially simple, holy priest—a side of Monsignor Knox I had not suspected until one day my neighbor brought for me to read a letter from Monsignor Vernon Johnson, who had seen Knox for the last time, scarcely a fortnight before death claimed him. In it he told of the dying priest's pain, his resignation to the Divine will, his eagerness to die.

At last, with the Waugh biography the portrait is for me complete. What I see now is the whole man. Sheer brilliance is always formidable, sometimes a little frightening. Here, however, is portrayed the work of grace during the years of maturity and full growth we needed to know about. It was this that made this great man what he really was, a priest after our Blessed Lord's own heart.

In an Anglican Seminary—January 11, 1962

Occasionally I am asked about the Anglican seminary from which I was graduated in 1933. Mine was the General Theological Seminary, the official school of theology of the Protestant Episcopal Church and an institution of graduate study that has enjoyed since its founding in 1819 pre-eminence among schools of its kind. I ought perhaps to make clear that it bears little resemblance to its counterparts in America, the schools that train the sectarian Protestant clergy. Although the late war brought to the seminary an increased enrollment, a new and less parochial outlook than it had had before, and on the whole a student body far superior to that of my day, these changes have not substantially altered its life and work. Here, if anywhere, the French proverb applies: *Plus ça change, plus c'est la même chose.*

Situated in old Chelsea on New York's lower West side, the seminary occupies a city block now almost completely bounded by its library residences, and chapel. Entering from Ninth Avenue, you come into a well-tended close and for all the world you might be in an English quad at Oxford or Cambridge. Here you see clusters of students in academic gown, for the dress is secular and the wearing of the gown to lectures and "in hall" obligatory. Right out of an English novel is the young don, or Fellow, his gown billowing in the breeze on his way to his lecture. Or coming down the walk is the venerable professor, the amiable divine, whose latest witticism is on every tutor's lips. In his early days Newman would have been no stranger here. The tone and atmosphere are more academic than clerical and nothing more unlike the Catholic seminary could be imagined.

We were so far in advance of our time as to have the English tutorial system and the seminar as the normal means of instruction. Professors lectured on their subjects at two hour sessions once a week. But it was to our tutor that we reported. He assigned our reading and listened (how patiently!) to our weekly paper, a long and serious essay formally presented, the result of what small skill in research and expression we were acquiring. No method of teaching and learning I know of is superior to this, for it demands the reading of primary sources, independent research, and original thinking. Needless to add, it requires of the tutor and lecturer creative teaching of the first order. And this we had.

If in my day the teaching of systematic theology left much to be desired, this want of completeness was more than made up by the peerless courses in the Old and New Testament. As austere as inwardly burning as the Prophets themselves, our dean was their interpreter, the only human being, a friend once confessed to me, he was ever afraid of. A renowned scholar, Dean [Hughell] Fosbroke lectured masterfully, which meant that to his great and deep learning he brought the use of majestic language. To this day I turn to his notes, taken for the most part word for word, and read them for sheer pleasure. "The Dean on the Psalms"—the phrase was a colloquialism—is someone and something to remember. For the New Testament we had the then ranking scholar of the non-Catholic world. I shall never cease to be grateful for my years at the feet of these men.

"But what was the life like?" you may be asking. I should like to tell you of this at another time.

Two Great and Gentle Men—July 18, 1963

It was cheering news indeed to Father Reinhold's hosts of friends, admirers and readers to learn a few months ago of his (I would say, miraculous) recovery resulting from a new type of surgery to which in his extremity he submitted. One in his pitiable condition would, I should suppose, have done anything since, whatever the results, his situation could hardly have been worse than it was.

Anyway, Father Reinhold is the first of these two great and gentle men. (I would have written "priests" had there been room in the title.) My debt to him is incalculable. For many years as an Anglican I knew him through his writings, especially his tract in *Orate Fratres*, the forerunner of today's *Worship*. Here, I realized, was someone whose language I understood; someone who like me must have been trained to approach every subject, and especially the liturgy, by the historical method, for much that he said echoed the material and the research learned and pursued at my Anglican seminary. Here was a priest who wrote clearly, simply, always refreshingly, and who was invariably challenging and exciting to read.

When, therefore, the time came to talk with a Catholic priest, his was the first name to come to my mind. In June of 1948 I left New York for the West Coast where Reinhold was then pastor. If I had jitters at the thought of knocking at a rectory door of fears of this priest's magisterial manner—I had pictured him as reserved and schoolmasterish—these were dispelled when he met me at the threshold; young for his years, gracious, in those days still an active sportsman, a gentleman to his fingertips, Father Reinhold was the epitome of friendliness and charm.

The only apparent riches in his humble, jerry-built rectory were his books—shelf after shelf lining every available space downstairs. Here was the home of a student, or rather, a trained scholar without a trace of pedantry or pretense. We talked far into the night, I making the best case I could for Anglicanism. His remark as we said good night was characteristic of him, as his friends will at once recognize: "You don't mean," he said at the foot of the stairs, "that to all the unpopular causes I espouse I must add Anglicanism! Oh, dear me!"

Next day we left by motor for points east, for Father had a commitment in New York the following week. Our immediate objective, however, was Saint Louis where, according to his insistence, I had to meet Monsignor Hellriegel and see Holy Cross.

Bedraggled, dirty, travel-ridden and exhausted after more than 400 miles' driving that Sunday, we sat down to Monsignor's table in the most hospitable rectory I have ever seen. The best lager was brought out and quantities of German bread, spiced meats, and pastries. Never, I think, was a hot tub more welcome nor an old-fashioned brass bedstead more all-enfolding: Monsignor knew well what the wayfaring pilgrim most needed at that point! Refreshed and excited, I was up next day in good season for the Community Mass.

I write of these great and gentle priests because, under God, they were, to use a theological term, a proximate cause of my coming to the Church.

Anticipating the Dialogue—July 25, 1963

It is, and was then, impossible to define my state of mind when I sought out a Catholic priest. Certainly I could not have said then that I would not some day forsake the Anglican position; but neither was I then able to renounce it. Friends and confidants were of little use to me because I resisted their pressure on me to remain and, besides, I knew well all that they had to say to me, for I had been saying it to myself for years. All I knew was that ultimately doubt must be resolved one way or the other: but how? and when? and in whose favor?

If anyone thinks that such a state of mind is easy to live with, he is much deceived. Besides the struggle within, I had a cure of souls; and whereas I knew I was not the indispensable man, nevertheless I could not walk out on people who depended on me.

Both Reinhold and Hellriegel were in those days far in advance of their times. They anticipated by many years the current spirit of the "dialogue." I mean that without compromise of their own principles they helped me toward and understanding of the Church and made every possible effort to understand me—all in the spirit, as Cardinal Bea would insist, of the utmost charity.

I had expected the kind of pressure I got from my co-religionists, but of this there wasn't so much as a little finger's weight. In fact, their first words were, in effect, "Relax, Father. Nothing is ever truly resolved under tension. Of course you don't know how or when or even whether so crucial a step as this is going to be taken. Only God knows the outcome."

The idea, then, was to go back to New York and in good faith to go about my work. Many—oh, very many on both sides—would have urged immediate withdrawal from all official duties; many on both sides would have accused me—and some on my side did—of duplicity. But that is not the view these two men took, for with me they agreed that a vacuum in the life of the mind and spirit is perilous: "seven other demons more wicked than the first"—these could well enter and dwell in me, so that my latter state would be worse than the first! This I believed and to hear it from them brought immeasurable comfort and strength.

"Go back, Father, to your work and your people." Some will—some did—say that this was more clever than Christian, more subtle than the charity I took it for. But I disown this kind of suspicion and cynicism, because and accusation like this ill comports with the granite character of these men. I felt this intuitively: "by their fruits shall ye know them."

The links they forged for the chain of succeeding events were of purest gold. "If," they said, "or when the time comes, get in touch with Father Damasus" (then at Regina Laudis, which in time became my first home as a Catholic). The time came and I did. And how shall I ever speak of him and what he did for me with appreciation due? And he in turn brought me to Father Stack; and Father Stack to the Archbishop of Hartford; and so the chain was forged, link by link, to this very present and happiest of days.

As an Anglican friend said then and would, I feel sure, say again today: "God directed you to the best there is; they don't come any finer."

A Democratic Community—November 12, 1965

I have seen true democracy at work in the Catholic Church. I have seen, too, what appears to be the nearly ideal human society, one whose principles could furnish a guide for other Christian societies. I am thinking especially the parish and the family. Perhaps you recall an essay in this place last summer about St. Benedict's principle, "obedience to one another." Well, I saw this in practice at Mount Saviour.

In this community the only distinction between the lay monk and the priest is one of function and not of rank. That is to say, men are advanced to the priesthood not as a matter of course, but as they are needed to serve the demands of the community. What counts at Mount Saviour, as indeed what was foremost in the mind of St. Benedict, is the monastic life itself—in a word, family life. So that a young man entering this community aspires to this and not necessarily to the priesthood. Indeed, as was the custom in St. Benedict's time, all monks are addressed as "Father," with the result that one identifies those who are priests only as he sees them vested for Mass or for the giving of the Sacraments.

When my friend and I were there, both the prior and subprior were absent. The next in line of authority—and this determined by the years spent in solemn vows—was a Father John. Father John is a lay monk and, as it happens, the head farmer—young, rugged, a tireless worker, possessed of a glorious voice. It was a sight to see him come in from the barn to preside at the noonday office in choir. Over his farm pants and boots he wore the short monastic work tunic complete with cowl. Occupying the chief place in the choir, he was the officiant at all the offices and at meals he presided from the head table. Everybody here waits on everybody else, the priests on the lay monks and these on the priests without distinction or favor. A wonderful object lesson, this, in the simple give and take of family life—"obedience to one another," or, as St. Paul put it, "preferring one another in honor." As I watched this I could not but recall how Ronald Knox, at one point in his priestly career, got himself released from the faculty of a seminary because one (and an elegant) bill of fare was served at the priests' table and another (and poorer one) at the students' tables. And I remembered my shock when I became aware of this practice at Baltimore. Naive man that I was, it took me about three weeks to catch on this. And fortunately for me, I found it vastly amusing. An essentially bourgeois behavior, it has in my view no place in our society. Doubtless it has long since been scrapped in our seminaries. It is American, and it is Christian, to "share and share alike."

Father Damasus, the prior of Mount Saviour, makes much of the advantage of discussion among and with the members of his monastic family. In his latest news letter he writes: "Perhaps the most noteworthy development in our community life is the emergence of group work and group discussions. After less than a year, community discussions have become an immemorial custom we can hardly remember or imagine life without them." This brings to mind my own experience in teaching boys. At the beginning of each year I used to say something like this: "Every boy in this class is free to express his opinion about any book we read this year. His opinion may be ill-formed and immature, in which case we shall try to round it out and supply what is wanting. But the important thing is, have an idea, make a judgment, and feel free to express it. We shall listen, and we shall respect what you have to say." Never in my experience were the lines of communication between class and teacher closed; always there was mutual respect and mutual trust. For the life of me I do not see how families, or even parish families, can flourish in Christian love without this kind of "dialogue," this essential give-and-take, between father and family, between priest and people.

Reflection on all the foregoing has sent me back to our Christian ministries were a hierarchy, to be sure; but they were a hierarchy not of rank, not of honor, but of function. The God-Man himself came, he said, not to be "ministered to, but to minister." His vicar on earth enjoys no more sublime distinction than that of being "the servant of the servants of God." And who among us can mediate long enough on the example given in the "new commandment" on that first Holy Thursday night—the washing by the Son of God of the feet of the sons of men?

Looking Back on Retreat—September 24, 1965

It has been a good retreat here at Mount Saviour, so good indeed that it has ended too soon for both my priest-companion and me. (Of how few retreats in my life can I say that?) Here were peace and both intellectual and spiritual refreshment in nearly perfect balance, the only noise being the Mohawk jets to and from nearby Corning airport and the hum of the milking machines in the new cow parlor. There were quantities of all the (for me) wrong sorts of food—bread in abundance from the Trappist bakeries at Our Lady of the Genesee, no meal, in fact scarcely a protein in sight—but no matter: this indulgence is already under correction, I was glad to see a company of young priests on retreat or simply visiting, observing, and learning. For Mount Saviour is surely the place today for the young in mind; it is preeminently a workshop and school for those of us from the outside who would study the liturgy and the current renewal under the best possible conditions.

My dear friends, the Prior and sub-Prior, were absent—Father Damasus in Rome and Father Gregory away giving a retreat. This was a disappointment as I had many questions to ask and much to learn from them both. Twice a day, however, we had taped conferences, and one of these was by Father Damasus. It was good to hear his voice again as he shared with us his vast knowledge and deep love of the Scriptures and the Fathers of the Church. The ethos of Mount Saviour is profoundly biblical and patristic; against this essential background the life of worship and of the sacraments is set. What one sees and hears and experiences is the Christian life of community lived as nearly ideally as one can conceive it on this planet. But you have to go there and live it for however brief a time to know what I mean. I have not the words to convey it.

The monastery is a church "in the round" with three bays serving as antechapels for visitors. These extend like radii from the center where stands the massive stone altar. Here, every morning—for me the ending and the beginning of the day, sleep meanwhile having been merely a necessary interlude—is celebrated the community Mass. Six priests concelebrated with the principal celebrant. What a sight this was! Still ringing in my ears is the Prayer of the Faithful: the petitions were chanted and to each the community sang a harmonized "Lord, have mercy," humming the final chord through the chanting of the next petition. For the Ordinary of the Mass the *English Mass of Mount Saviour* (available, by the way, from the Gregorian Institute of America) was used—a simple, expressive, and brief setting which my dear children are going to learn as soon as we get copies for them. The sacrifice completed, there came the Communion procession.

If I bring away from this place a single impression that can affect my own ministry, it is this; that in principle nothing happens at the community Mass (except concelebration—and who knows we may have this boon in our parish churches one of these days) that cannot be brought in time to our people in our parishes. I feel that Mount Saviour is no ivory tower, no liturgical museum, no isolated refuge for perfectionists, but a community very like any other household of committed Christians serving God and one another in faith and charity. What I see and have been able to live here for a few days, I can help bring to my people.

Were I 30 years younger I would, I think, "make my oblation," as the saying is, at Mount Saviour. I wonder if I would have what it takes to be a son of St. Benedict; I like to think so. It would be a singular privilege to spend the better part of one's lifetime in a house where a noble tradition—surely the noblest and oldest continuing tradition in the Western Church is without loss or diminution fast accommodating itself to the challenges and the needs of the Church of our time. St. Benedict must smile with favor these sons of his wise in the wisdom of the Christian ages, yet as up to date as today.

3

The Great Church and Ecumenism

THE CHURCH CAN BE itself only when the competing, opposing, and condemning denominations come together to *be* the resurrected Christ. For Gordon, of course, Catholicism was both the means and the goal of this coming together. In a striking column, written at the end of his *Transcript* career, he proposed the church as the resurrected, real, and mystical body of Christ. Instead of arguing historicity, we must meditate this reality. Analyzing the primitive church, its later history, and his own experiences, he set himself to propose and propagate this "great church," the label created by the saint and theologian of the second century, Bishop Irenaeus of Lyon, to signify the universal, all embracing apostolic faith community established by Christ.

This community today will celebrate the Eucharist in both splendid and austere ceremonies; everyone will share in the selection of bishops and pastors, bishops will share governing charism with their priests, parish priests will be free to marry and pursue secular occupations compatible with ministry, and the lay diaconate will be restored.

The bringing together of the separated churches into the one great church is the task of ecumenism, and Gordon shared his dreams of ultimate success and his suffering, as the efforts faltered, picked up ever so slowly, and continued on—sometimes inflected by false optimism. At one and the same time, he praises John Henry Newman for his love of the Anglicanism he left behind and takes himself to task for insufficient appreciation of the

Protestants around him and isolation from fellow Episcopalians who didn't share his theological views. Even so, Protestant churches have failed to live up to their own mission: to wit, the book-length criticisms of the Presbyterian theologian Geddes MacGregor, who believed that Protestantism deserved more criticism than Rome for having ignored the reality of the Church, ideals of spiritual perfection, and the power of the liturgy.

Gordon naturally was preoccupied by, and pleased by, the reforming efforts in the Anglican/Episcopal Churches and devoted frequent columns to events, writings, and personalities, emphasizing their social consciousness: ministries to the London slums and the poor in the old British colonies, promotion of labor reforms, contemporary "freedom riders," and ecumenical gatherings in the United States. He was especially taken with the pronouncements of Arthur Lichtenberger, presiding bishop of the Episcopal Church, the Archbishops of Canterbury, Geoffrey Fisher and Michael Ramsey, and the achievements of his close friends, the Episcopal bishops, Kilmer Myers and Paul Moore. He saw promise of Episcopal unity in the liturgical celebrations that brought together low, middle, and high churchmen in a Eucharistic apostolate intimately tied to Christian witness. He reported the uniquely beautiful Eucharistic celebrations at the Episcopal church of St. Mary the Virgin and the cathedral of St. John the Divine, the Archbishop of Canterbury, Michael Ramsey concelebrating with numerous priests in the first celebration and attended to by major representatives of the Catholic archbishop of New York in the second one. Gordon recalled also the charismatic ministries and forthright social reform position of his friends Myers and Moore, Myers declaring he would rejoice to have the Pope as his holy father also—should both churches arrive at the level of charity which would make it possible.

He reported how Catholic and Episcopal religious communities offered mutual hospitality and shared in one another's services—virtually always short of taking communion together. In the United States, the Anglican community of Holy Cross dedicated their new chapel with many Catholic monks and religious in attendance, and the Catholic Benedictines of Mount Saviour Monastery warmly welcomed Anglican Benedictines in communal sharing. Earlier on, in England during World War II, according to the report of Gordon's friend, the renowned Anglican Benedictine scholar, Gregory Dix, the two communities initiated participating in one another's sharing of community life.

After the Second Vatican Council, the European churches quickly moved forward in common-worship experiments, especially in the Netherlands; in America they were much slower. Home in Connecticut, Gordon participated occasionally in meetings and celebrations, chagrined by his obligation to explain why he could not pray with Congregational youth and adults at one point, rejoicing in the down-to-earth Methodist witness at another. His admiration of John and Charles Wesley is virtually unbounded: making the Eucharist available and bringing energetic preaching to the poor in cities and the countryside ignored by other Anglicans. John Wesley broke with tradition by ordaining his own clergy, but he created a style of ministry that—brought to America—transformed the Christian landscape there.

As the years went on, Gordon permitted himself to wonder if he might, in fact, have remained an Episcopal priest in the lively ecumenical post-Vatican II culture of his later years! The irony is that if ecumenism is successful, conversion is not necessary.

Christ Crucified, Risen—April 12, 1968

During their lifetime the Eleven (to whose company Matthias was added) based their claim to be apostles to their having seen the risen Lord and, as the word "apostle" implies, on their having been sent out to preach the good news of Christ's victory over death. Thus, when St. Paul, to the wonder of the infant Church, claimed apostleship, he justified his claim by invoking the same test: he, too, on the way to Damascus, saw Christ plain and was then and there commissioned to preach him crucified and risen. This he did for the remaining years of his life.

"Some man will ask," he wrote in his first letter to the Christians at Corinth, "how are the dead raised up and with what body do they come?" And he tells us. We cannot say that we know nothing about the resurrection body. We know far more than we at first suppose, granting always that the mystery is unfathomable. St. Paul gives us four adjectives, and these provide a key to our understanding. The new body in Christ is risen, spiritual, incorruptible, and glorious.

It is a risen body. But here, right away, we meet a difficulty: not by all who saw Christ risen, nor at once by them, was he recognized. Not until he spoke to her did Mary Magdalene know him, you recall. And you remember how on that evening walk to Emmaus the two disciplines talked to our Lord and yet how, also, not until he broke bread with them, did they "know" him. Critics and scholars of the New Testament tell us that it was the Eucharist and the continuing presence of the Spirit among the early Christians that gave proof of the "on going" life of Christ. I was brought up on this view; and yet, there is always the claim, "We have seen the Lord!" Whatever this means, it means that there was in these men and women a conviction that Christ was alive; that they were in vital touch with him.

The risen body is spiritual. And whatever that may mean (because it is a contradiction) it means this: that this body is no longer subject to the laws of physics and chemistry, no longer bound by time and space.

It is an incorruptible body. What was "sown" in corruption is "raised" incorruptible. What could suffer pain and bleed to death is now beyond the ordinary frailty and ravages of our mortal frame. Nothing can anymore injure it; nothing limits it any longer.

It is a glorious body. Yet, though glorified, it bears the marks of its passage through this world, the marks of the "passing over" from pain and death to the grave, and beyond. The wounds of life's struggle to the death are not hid but made glorious by "transfiguration."

There is one more "mark" of the risen Christ which St. Paul did not mention—unless, that is, all his preaching bore witness to it—and that is this: that the risen Christ is seen, too, in the continuing presence and life of the Christian community. Spirit-indwelt, daily nourished by the Eucharist, the Christian body, the Church was then, is now, and will be until the end of time, the sign of the risen, on-going life of Christ beyond the grave. Here, in the beloved community, the Church, yesterday, today, and always, is the sign supreme of the risen Christ. If you need "proof" that Christ is risen, here it is in your midst: you and I and all the fellowship of the baptized are that sign, for we are his body alive in his world. This is all we really know, in the only world we really know, and it is perhaps all that we need to know. One thing is certain: it makes out duty plain, to be that body!

The Coming 'Great Church'—January 13, 1967

Rarely, at such ecumenical gatherings as I manage to attend, does someone not ask the question, "What will the reunited Christian Church look like?" To this, last Sunday night's meeting in New Britain was no exception. (It was an enthusiastic gathering of two neighboring churches at the invitation of one of our men's clubs.) "What form will the 'Great Church' take?

someone asked. It is always a good question, one that is foremost in people's minds, and one on which it is fascinating to speculate.

The answer I give is this: that the truly Ecumenical Church—"ecumenical" because truly and visibly one, and truly worldwide—could conceivably, as far as the West is concerned, will resemble nothing so much as the Church of the fourth century, in appearance, in structure, in creedal commitments. (As for the last-named, the Faith will not have changed, but it will have undergone radical restatements.) And turning to my fellow-panelist, the young minister of the guest congregation, I asked, "Could you be happy, should such a development take place, in the Church of the Augustine or an Ambrose or a Gregory?" His answer was plainly affirmative and this I found heartening.

This church will be "primitive in its purity and simplicity as was the Church of the "golden age" and yet also as contemporary and as vital as today itself. Why do I think this? Because already, in the current liturgical reform, the lineaments of the classic age can easily be discerned. Visit, for example, the new Church of the Resurrection in Wallingford—the best thing I have seen yet; it is not hard to see Augustine himself presiding from the chair in that gloriously open and spacious sanctuary. Or, attend the Eucharist at the Montfort Seminary: the austerity of the rite in that unadorned Upper Room, the plainness of the vesture, the directness with which words are spoken and sung and actions done—these restore to the Roman rite, the incomparable Roman rite, for such was its genius and glory before it was subjected to the misfortunes of history, of the medieval, and, worse, the baroque periods. And here our interest is not antiquity for antiquity's sake. (Any discerning collector of antiques learns sooner or later that because something is old, it is not necessarily good.) No, our interest is rather in those forms which best make present to us today the Eucharist (the very heart of the matter) as assembly, as anamnesis (i.e., commemorative sacrifice), and as sacrificial meal. With this recovery—and may God speed it!—will disappear all the regal circumstance, all the window dressing, all the pretense and pomp that had come, until recently, and erroneously, to be equated with Catholic worship.

It is not unthinkable that in the truly Ecumenical Church, the people will once again, as in the great past, have a voice in the selection of their bishops and pastors. The diaconate will inevitably (and rather sooner than later, I think) be restored to its ancient dignity, and this because it will have quickly become an urgent necessity for the life of the Church. Bishops will be restored to their traditional functions as "priests ordained to ordain;" as real shepherds (of small and, I suspect, poor dioceses!) visiting as once they did and knowing their flocks parish by parish, Sunday by Sunday; and as the pre-eminent teachers and homilists of their dioceses. The parish clergy, not inconceivably, by that day may be free to marry and many if not most may by then be supplementing their stipends in pursuing, alongside the men in their parishes, secular occupations. For my own part, I can foresee in all this nothing but gain for Christendom.

Well, by now many of you will have had your fill of my crystal-gazing. But so far, I like what I see and shall continue to stare, entranced. My moments of rapt concentration are interrupted now and then by cries from some of you of "Never! Never!" But "never" I remind you, is a long, long, time indeed—so long that I rarely use the word.

With Conversion, New Grace—December 13, 1962

Lest some readers think the writer soft of heart or worse, soft in the head, for his distress at having to part with his Protestant friends at their church door, something may be said in his defense. It is this: that with his conversion came a new grace, something up to that time unfelt, and that was a completely new attitude toward those outside the Church. Pity is not the word, for that sounds smug. The prophets would have described it as a "yearning" over them, a great desire to reach out to them and take them by the hand and lead them to the fullness of grace, and above all, to show them the Church as one as he himself come to know it.

Someone remarked about Newman that he was much more tender toward Anglicanism, much more solicitous for Anglicans, and much more aware of their good faith after his conversion than before. That is something of what I mean here. Something happened to you: the scales fall from your eyes and you see as you did not see before; you sense the poverty of your former state and you long to share the riches you now have with those you left behind.

It was not always thus with me, as I have implied. Through all my Anglican ministry I kept aloof from all but my little clique of like-minded Anglicans. Ultra-parochial. I wore blinders and saw not right nor left but only the path through Anglicanism I had chosen. As for Protestants of the Calvinist or Wesleyan or Lutheran persuasions, I knew none nor wanted to.

When I said that it is nearly impossible to satisfy Protestants with the answer to their question, "Why cannot Catholics take part in our services?" I meant that, try as he will, one leaves them bewildered, even perhaps hurt. The answer we give presupposes so much that they cannot possibly take in, so much that there is not time to develop in one brief encounter, that I always feel at a loss.

The reason the question is difficult is this: Protestants, always excepting many well-taught Anglicans, have all but lost any notion of the Church as a divine society, given from above, divinely and solely commissioned to represent and speak for God and in turn to offer him the worship that befits his majesty. They think of the Church—any church, their own—as a voluntary gathering of sympathetic and like-minded persons, autonomous (you sometimes see the word "free" in their title and this means freedom from any sort of hierarchical control) and exercising only such authority as will reflect and represent their own religious aspirations and activities, Thus, one such "democratic" and "free" association is as good as another: all are equally agreeable to God and the individual can choose that religious society which best corresponds to his personal needs and tasted in matters of religion. This eminently unhistorical, untraditional, certainly unscriptural view of the Church results in a subjective and sentimental appraisal of our claims to be the Church.

Hence, the invariable impression we create is this: "He thinks we're not good enough . . . or that God hears only the prayers of those who use certain words and go through certain forms . . . or that our ministers are God's second class citizens"—and all this is painful to read on their faces.

It is not that I yearn to attend, much less participate in, Calvinist services. I didn't in the Anglican days and I have no desire to do so now— and for all the right and defensible reasons. Rather, I make a distinction between this and the occasions like the one I described last week. This is nothing formal or official about the devotions that precede or follow these conversations; if one is approving anything, it is simply prayer in common.

Nor can I get rid of the notion in my head that somewhere, sometime, only the dear Lord knows how much later, some person is going to remember the evening a priest addressed his group and stayed to pray. He may even be impressed then and there, like the man in my village who, last year when I talked to his group of adults, wrote me next day. These, believe it or not, were his words: "You have completely changed for the better my view of the Catholic Church and of Catholics." How I prize that letter!

A Reformed Protestantism—December 28, 1961

My Anglican friend who brought me *The Coming Reformation* said, as he handed it to me, "This will interest you. The author, a Protestant, says that if the Reformers were to come back today, they would be more at home in your Church than in one of their own." This was invitation enough for me. I read the book at one sitting.

Dr. Geddes MacGregor, a Scot of Scots if names mean anything, is a Presbyterian minister and currently Professor of Theology at the University of Southern California. He has the boldness of youth (I judge him to be a few years this side of forty) and his convictions are cast in strong language indeed. He is no mean scholar, for his book testifies to a wide reading of traditional theology, of Catholic spirituality, and of the history of Christian liturgy. I imagine that the Protestant who reads him, if he is not outraged, will be stirred to his depths and at the same time hard put to it to explain away or defend the weaknesses of his position. Dr. MacGregor confines his observations of Protestantism to the Calvinist heritage. His book is a merciless excoriation. No admirer of Rome, he is hard on us, but he is harder on his own.

Protestantism, he says, has failed and is failing utterly today because it has proved false to the Reformation. So true is this that Calvin would find no slightest resemblance in the Protestant churches to his idea of "the Church reformed." In fact, he would disown this allegedly "reformed" religion as a sham and a fraud. (Remember, this is the author speaking, not I.)

The bankruptcy of Protestantism is evident to MacGregor on two counts. The first is the abject failure of Protestantism to nurture in its adherents a sense of "the reality of the Church." Not only is there no compelling doctrine of the Body of Christ, but there is no conviction in the Protestant of an overruling guardianship by the Church in matters crucial to his salvation. Indeed, asks the author, how can there be when from Sunday to Sunday houses of worship are tight shut, when, even on the Lord's Day, the atmosphere is drab, stuffy, and barren of devotion; when public worship is a travesty, a shocking display of bourgeois mediocrity and shallow sentimentality?

Second, the ideal of Christian perfection, of holiness as indispensable to the life of the Christian society—this, too, has all but disappeared among Protestants. There is no understanding of the traditional Christian disciplines, no knowledge of the principles of the interior life in their place has been put the pursuit at best of "a second-class ideal," a lower aim for the majority. Here he dwells a length on Kierkegaard's famous contrast between the worldly Catholic prelate and the equally worldly Lutheran bishop. Be the former ever so corrupt, there is always for the possibility of having the shadow of a mendicant friar cross his path. He can never forget that there exist the evangelical counsels of poverty, chastity, and obedience. Not so, however, the Lutheran, for with him these ideals have been lost sight of. Here MacGregor is at his best. To use the psalmist's metaphor, the zeal of his house has all but eaten him up. But it makes sad reading.

Three things, then, the author foresees in the "coming reformation" of Protestantism: recovery of the doctrine of the Church, revival of traditional discipline, and spirituality, and a rebirth of Catholic liturgy. But to all this we ask: when these things shall have been rediscovered and restored, what becomes of Protestantism?

A Thirst for Justice—September 28, 1961

If we would understand the best of the Anglicans better, we need to realize that much that is vital among them is supplied by their passion for social righteousness. This thirst for justice is a direct contribution of the Oxford Movement. It has by now permeated as in fact it distinguishes the public witness of Anglicanism at its best.

It was in the 1860s that the ideas of the first generation of the Oxford reformers were wrested from the purely academic and carried out to the pastoral and parochial *milieu*. The heroes of that day were the men who brought the good news of Christ to the docks of London, to the slums of Birmingham and Manchester, to the poor and hungry and outcast wherever they found them. These men put to shame the typical Anglican parson of the preceding century and a half—the butt of the novelist and playwright, the hunting parson, the hunter of the drawing rooms of the high born and the privileged.

A social consciousness thus became the hall-mark of the "catholic-minded" Anglican. Listen, for example, to the young colonial bishop of Zanzibar, Frank Weston, addressing a congress in London in 1918. "You cannot claim to worship Jesus in the tabernacle if you do not pity Jesus in the slum . . . It is folly, it is madness, to suppose that you can worship Jesus on his throne of glory when you are sweating him in the bodies and souls of his children. Go out into the highways and hedges and look for him in the ragged and naked, in the oppressed and sweated, in those who have lost hope, and those who are struggling to make good. Look for Jesus in them, and when you have found him, gird yourself with his towel of fellowship and wash his feet in the person of his brethren."

It was Frank Weston, by the way, who in the name of that same congress sent the following telegram to Pope Benedict XV: "Sixteen thousand Anglo-Catholics in congress assembled offer respectful greetings to the Holy Father, humbly praying that the day of peace may quickly break." He died in 1924 at fifty-three. His words and outlook, alas!, are far from typical of the Anglican hierarchy and in his day they made "no small stir."

His legacy and that of his kind has been what I have called this thirst for righteousness in the social order. It is reflected in the work of such eminent women as the late Mary Kingsbury Simkhovich, who pioneered in the founding of settlement houses in the slums of New York, and Frances Perkins, whose zeal from labor reforms in New York anticipated by many years her appointment to Mr. Roosevelt's cabinet. Both of these women learned their doctrine of social justice under the aegis of the Episcopal Church.

Thus it was no surprise to me to open my paper the other day and find the names of thirty or more of the Episcopal clergy among the "freedom riders." Ill-timed and rash though some have deemed their witness to be, these men have (as they see it) inherited the privilege of being uncomfortable in the pursuit of their convictions. This I know because among them are two of my friends. You will not misunderstand me when I say that for them and what they are doing I have unqualified admiration, even as I know they admire our great army of missionaries the world over and the noble company of Catholic martyrs of the present time.

Liturgical Life Brings Unity—June 24, 1965

My Anglican friend in New York reported to me by telephone on the 1965 Liturgical Conference held last April under the aegis of the Episcopal diocese of New York. He followed this by sending his diocese paper which carried a full report and a few glorious pictures. The opening service and all the meetings were held in the ballroom of the Waldorf. The final service as held in the Cathedral of St. John the Divine.

At the opening service an English bishop concelebrated with 12 of the diocesan clergy. Communion was distributed at 12 "stations" in the ballroom. The congregation received standing. Some three-score of our priests, I understand, registered for the sessions as observers and auditors.

What interests me is that in the picture of the concelebrating clergymen, most of whom I knew in the old days, I can identify men who in my time would have been called "low churchmen" and who, I think it safe to say, would not have been interested in such a demonstration as this one. Present also were some "high churchmen" and these, too would not have been enthusiastic about such an obvious erasing of "party" lines.

Time was when one could say that, like all Gaul, Anglicanism was divided into three parts—low, broad, and high. Adherents of "low Church" gloried in their Protestant heritage, talked of "ministry" rather than "priesthood," and eschewed any and all of the trappings of Rome. Those of the "broad Church" persuasion represented a liberal, undogmatic churchmanship, their primary interest being good works rather than orthodoxy. The "high Church" clergy insisted in the Catholic notes of the Anglican Church, and many (the very "High") were openly pro-Roman, if not in theology, then certainly in matters ceremonial. We used to recite a little jingle, to wit: "low and lazy; broad and hazy; high and crazy."

There were degrees of "highness", as the designation "very High" suggests. If you were "very High" you did all the things that Roman liturgical scholars were praying that Rome would give up. (We have lived to see the day!) The scale of "highness" went from the use of moderate ceremonial and a "full" service to a frenzy of ceremonial and quasi-Roman behavior, but these "parties" and their difference are, it seems, fast disappearing. Men of all shades of belief and practice regard this as a good thing. They delight in their new-found sense of unity, understanding, and tolerance. It was apparent that they are committed to liturgical renewal in their own church. They are aware that for this they have at hand an incomparable liturgy, of whose genius and beauty they seem to be making the most these days.

They are discovering that liturgy is life, and not mere fancy dress and still fancier behavior. They are realizing, all of them together, that out of liturgical life come, quite naturally and inevitably, a sense of Christian brotherhood and its necessary concomitant, Christian social action. (This is a lesson that we and our people have yet to learn.) At their conference on liturgy not one syllable was spoken about vestments or ceremonies of "how we do it in my parish." Rather, every speaker stressed the crucial need for Christians to go forth from the Eucharist and bear witness in the world. The visiting bishop put it this way: "Words without action can reduce love to a sham. God will judge us not by the accuracy of our ritual, but by the impact we make on out world after the Eucharist is over." This reminds me very much of the dismissal used at Maryknoll: "Go: now live the Mass." All this is bearing fruit; the "time lag" has caught up, so to speak, there is among Anglicans a common ground for Eucharistic life and Christian witness.

Here, too, is fresh and fertile ground from greater understanding between these Christians and ourselves. We have much to teach them, and they learn from us most eagerly. But so, too, is there much that we can learn from them.

These Are Hopeful Signs—February 1, 1962

The Oxford English Dictionary has this to say of "Bravo." "(ancestry. Italian. Bravo, superlative bravissimo, also used.) Capital! Well done! Hence, a cheer."

A friend has sent me a longish clipping from *The American Church News*, the official magazine of the American Church Union whose membership both clerical and lay comprises most of the Episcopalians of Anglo-Catholic sympathies in this country. The excerpt is a report of the visit of courtesy paid last autumn by the Most Reverend Arthur C. Lichtenberger, Presiding Bishop of the Protestant Episcopal Church, to Pope John XXIII. Giving information which did not appear in the newspapers, it also corrects details erroneously reported both in secular and religious journals.

After celebrating a Communion service in Rome's Anglican church of St. Paul, Bishop Lichtenberger drove to the Vatican in a car provided by the U.S. naval attaché. Msgr. [Johannes] Willebrands, Secretary of the Vatican Commission on Unity, rode with him and the other members of his party, Bishop Lauriston L. Scaife of Western New York, an acknowledged authority on the Oriental churches, and Mr. Clifford P. Morehouse, a layman prominent in the affairs of the Episcopal Church.

The report continues: "Approaching the Pope's private library, after receiving the salutes of the Swiss Guards, the whole party waited while the Presiding Bishop has a private audience with the Pope, accompanied only by Msgr. Cardinale, who acted as interpreter. Entering the library, in purple cassock with pectoral cross, Bishop Lichtenberger was greeted warmly by the Pope who stood and clasped the bishop's hands in his saying, 'Bravo, bravo!'" Capital! Well done! Thus we all echo the Pope's enthusiastic cheer!

The meeting lasted 40 minutes and the conversation was, in Bishop Lichtenberger's words, "warm, friendly, and unrestrained." (How often, in accounts, of audiences with our Holy Father, the words "warm" and "friendly" occur!) Each asked questions and the Pope expressed keen interest in the then forthcoming conference at New Delhi, promising to pray for it.

After the private audience the Pope met the other members of the party. Gifts were exchanged. Those from the Anglican side were a crystal paperweight on which are etched the words. "More things are wrought by prayer than this world dreams of," and a copy of the American *Book of Common Prayer*, which the Pope, a student of English, promised to read.

The headlines in our morning papers are depressing enough. But occasionally, as with this most happy incident, a word of cheer goes out to all the world. These are hopeful signs—the only hopeful ones I read in our world today. I had in the old days a more than slight acquaintance with these three gentlemen. Bishop Lichtenberger came to the General Seminary to teach pastoral theology when I was a visiting lecturer in homiletics. Bishop Scaife was a class of two behind me. If the Presiding Bishop came away from the audience with Pope John, as he says, "with a great lift after being in his presence," I feel sure that the Holy Father was in his turn not unimpressed.

It Is a Timely Commitment—March 10, 1967

Dr. Geoffrey Fisher, when he was Archbishop of Canterbury, is said to have observed that united action by Christians, especially in the World Council of Churches, could become "a narcotic rather than a stimulant." Others have warned of this risk of euphoria, of an illusory elation that makes the real differences between and among us seem less crucial than they are.

Indeed, it is easy for a time to be this deceived. All of us who engage in ecumenical encounters have, I am sure, sensed this. Where the "two or three are gathered together" in Christ's name, there indeed he is present amid his presence through the Spirit is indeed real and to a degree felt. Everybody puts his best foot forward. Consideration for the other person, attention to his point of view, respect for his loyalties and convictions: all these uniquely ecumenical postures engender the best of good feeling. And we come away from these gatherings on a full tide of optimism and of hope. This I have felt, and so, I imagine, have many of you at one time or another.

For this reason, "the men who see things calmly," to use Cardinal Bea's characterization of the true ecumenist, are at pains to insist that our minds should never be dulled to the scandal of our divisions nor our wills allowed to grow weak in the sacrifices necessary for full reconciliation. If we do not feel keenly the pain of Christian disunity, we shall not have the incentive to persevere in our will and out striving to overcome it.

The Irish ecumenist, Father Michael Hurley, S. J. has applied this necessary discomfort to the ecumenical problem created by the mixed marriage of Christians. He suggests that in our conference with the partners to a marriage between Catholics and Protestants we should urge on them a totally new and timely commitment to give their union an ecumenical direction. Why, he asks, cannot the continuing pain of separation be made godly use of? Why must separation, even in the union of Christian marriage, necessarily cast a shadow on the marriage? Why, indeed, can it not be for the glory of God in so far as it forcibly reminds the husband and wife (and later, as God wills it, the parents of a growing Christian family) of the continuing disobedience of all Christians everywhere to God's will for the visible unity of his people?

For what is painfully true of the whole Christian world of our time—the tragedy of a Christendom divided, the effort to achieve unity under the Holy Spirit's guidance and the hope of its realization in God's good time: why cannot these be experienced in an uniquely poignant way in the family and the home? Daily prayers for the unity of God's people might thus be added to the customary family devotions. The same ecumenical postures and the good manners that prevail wherever we gather together in the cause of unity would acquire particular merit in the home. The mutual respect and consideration, with the understanding that results from these, would thus dominate the conduct of family life. What but enormous good could come of all this? For is not such a Christian family, even though for the time being divided in religion, in the words of St. John Chrysostom, a "little church"—the whole Christian world in microcosm?

Ecumenical Rites: So What?—October 27, 1967

On my table as I write are the orders of service for the two occasions early this month when Dr. Ramsey, Archbishop of Canterbury, was welcomed in New York. The first of these was the anniversary celebration of the dedication of the renowned Church of St. Mary the Virgin, in West 46th Street; the second, in the afternoon, at St. John's Cathedral, Morningside Heights. I should like to have been there, if only to meet hosts of old friends; but my mind's eye can see with fair accuracy, I think, what went on.

St. Mary's, a glorious building in the French Gothic style, was built early this century primarily as a setting in splendid functions. For years it has been the mecca of American "Anglo-Catholics"—a great showplace and the symbol of the Catholic revival in the Episcopal Church. But it was far more than this: under the rectorships of the famous Dr. [Joseph] Barry and of his successor, Dr. Mercer Williams of the Cowley Fathers, St. Mary's offered what I do not hesitate to claim was the finest teaching of Catholic doctrine and life, as well as the most expert confessional and pastoral direction of souls, as might be had anywhere in New York. These men were great teachers and superb confessors. Add to this a unique musical tradition—all the great baroque music was sung to near perfection, so much so that to St. Mary's were attracted New York's music lovers in hordes—and you have some idea of the contribution this landmark has made to the life of New York.

When Canterbury presided at this anniversary and welcoming service, no fewer than 18 clerics, many of whom had at one time served on the parish staff, concelebrated with the present rector. What a sight this must have been in the vast and suitably elevated sanctuary!

That same afternoon in St. John's was held "A Service Marking the Ecumenical Concern of the Episcopal Church in the Diocese of New York." Presiding with his guest, Dr. Ramsey, was the Bishop of New York, Dr. Donegan. In the great choir, my friend writes, among many Catholic priests, were Auxiliary Bishop Philip Furlong, representing Cardinal Spellman; Monsignor Myles Burke, pastor of nearby Corpus Christi Parish: and the ubiquitous Father Donahue of St. Patrick's Cathedral staff. Father Donahue appears to have some kind of official and roving ambassadorship, for my friend tells me he attends every ecumenical function and is greatly beloved of the Episcopal clergy. Dr. Carson Blake read the Scripture and Canterbury preached.

To all this there are some, representing all shades of pan-Christian spectrum, who will say, "So what?" Skeptical of the value of these great services, they shrug them off as beneath their attention. This, I think, is regrettable. For what these skeptics fail to realize is the enormous incentive to ecumenical concern these public witnesses afford lay people of all sorts of conditions and backgrounds. And when something of tremendous import is said by someone of tremendous importance (as was true that afternoon), this with the presence and cooperation in prayer of Christians of all groups and of the clergy of all churches, has unique and inestimable teaching power.

We Need a Holy Father—June 30, 1967

"Bravo!" thought I upon reading a couple of Sundays ago of Bishop C. Kilmer Myers' appeal to all non-Roman Catholic Christians to recognize the Pope as chief pastor of the universal church. It occurs to me that readers of this column may wish to know more about this remarkable (and still young) man than the national or religious press reports have furnished.

I first knew "Kim" Myers when he was a graduate student and tutor (equivalent to the English "don") at the General Seminary. I remember the afternoon he brought an enormous dog (I think it was an Afghan hound) to the Close to cheer his then celibate state and add one more picturesque creature to the company of seminary pets. It was a glorious summer afternoon, the feast of St. Vincent de Paul, 1947, and Paul and Jenny Moore were with us. The reason my memory is so vivid is Paul's remark that he has always been cheered by "Monsieur Vincent" because this great saint did not find his real and lasting work for the Lord until he was in his fifties. Anyway, Paul, now Suffragan Bishop of Washington, was about to move himself and his family to a Jersey City slum and there to pioneer in the work of the "inner city," where for some years he gained such knowledge and experience as today to place him among the giants of the movement for civil rights and racial justice. Myers soon left the academic life to do a similar job in New York's lower East Side. From there he went to Old Trinity's Chapel of the Intercession in Washington Heights, where he did a spectacular work of integrating the chapel and making it one of the chief centers of religious and cultural life in Manhattan. Meanwhile he married. There were no children of this union, so he and his wife took into the vicarage a Negro boy whom they had rescued from the streets. In a short time they adopted him and, later still, they added two more Korean war orphans to their family.

Alert readers of the press these few years past do not need to be reminded of Bishop Myers' forthright position on questions of domestic and international importance. He is not one to advance popular views. Not long after his consecration as bishop (he went, I seem to recall, to the Diocese of Michigan as its suffragan) he let his voice be heard with prophetic power on the rights of the worker and of the Negro in cities like Detroit and Lansing.

He has since been repeatedly and fearlessly outspoken in opposing our continuing involvement in Vietnam. And now, in San Francisco, where he succeeds Bishop Pike, he joins forces with the militant ecumenists. That was to be expected. For these matters are really all of a piece: justice at home, peace abroad, and the unity of Christians under the high priest he calls "the chief spokesman for the Christian community in the world."

Bishop Myers' successor at Intersession Chapel, and my very good friend, Dr. Leslie Lang, addressing a Communion breakfast at the invitation of a council of the Knights of Columbus in his neighborhood, said this: "We esteem and honor your Holy Father, just as we loved and revered his predecessor, Pope John. We would like to have Pope Paul as our Holy Father. But we shall not together with you have him as our Father in God and our chief Pastor until and unless we begin to behave towards one another as brothers and sisters of Christ's one family."

The Spirit Urges Us On—June 3, 1966

Caution, amounting to timidity, cripples both our prayer and our witness as sometimes to put us beyond the reach of the Spirit's promptings. We are very like the motorist who, seeing the way ahead clear and safe, and wishing to overtake the car in front of him, hesitates, then starts nosing out, and then loses courage, falling back again into line. The driver of the car ahead waves him on with frantic gestures: "Come ahead," he seems to call, "it's all clear, Come on!" But no: the timid soul is afraid to make the venture. So it is with us and the Holy Spirit. He motions, urges, encourages, points the way clear and safe ahead for us. But we hold back.

The Holy Cross News, Eastertide 1966, which I have through the kindness of a friend, reports on some exciting ecumenical exchanges between the (Episcopal) Order of the Holy Cross and their Roman Catholic brethren. Space allows me to report on only two of these; perhaps next week I can tell of the others.

The first is the occasion of the dedication of the new monastery at Holy Cross, West Park, N. Y. The Bishop of New York, Dr. Donegan, officiated at the blessing of the buildings and celebrated the Eucharist. Present in the chapel choir, alongside the monks of Holy Cross, were many of our religious from nearby communities Franciscans, Redemptorists, and (I am happy to make out in the picture) some of the Fathers and seminarians from our own Montfort Seminary, in Litchfield. There with the 600 or more guests they spent a day in friendship and prayer at what has been, there nearly 70 years past, a place of the warmest hospitality—and I should know, for I have often been there and to this day we owe much to it.

Then there is the account of an overnight visit by the Holy Cross postulants to our Benedictine Community at Mount Saviour, near Elmira. The master of postulants, Father Stevens, O.H.C., led the pilgrimage. He and his men, so runs the report, "were received as though they were another congregation of Benedictines. Both groups soon discovered a common life, and the spirit of brotherly love and the unifying periods of silence were so evident as almost to be felt."

What most touched me in this report were the words of Father Gregory, Mount Saviour's subprior, as he greeted the guests next morning at the community Eucharist. (I have known Father Gregory for 40 years, well and long enough to believe that his words spring from his heart.)

"As we approach the heart of the great mystery of our redemption in the Eucharist's Feast, I cannot tell you how deeply we grieve that we cannot invite you to be one with us in the receiving of our Lord's precious Body and Blood. Here it is that we should find our true unity. May our gracious God grant it to come soon. But even as we grieve, we know that there is a real unity among us in this moment of eternity: for we know that you, too, are grieving deeply that we cannot be at one in Holy Communion, though we share a common fellowship under Christ, our victorious King. We are at one, then, in love even now."

Thus, it is the religious on both sides—our own and the Anglican— who have the right place, the means, and the requisite courage to show us the way into the mystery of ecumenism. For them it appears to be a bold following of leadership, the urging-on, of the Holy Spirit. He says to them, "Come on! The way ahead is safe and clear." And they move out and ahead. For the rest of us, I sometimes think, the only way we will move forward is to have the Holy Spirit get behind us and push!

A Satisfactory Meeting—December 6, 1962

On a Sunday evening a few weeks ago I had the pleasure of meeting with the Pilgrim Fellowship of a nearby Congregational church. As you know, this fellowship corresponds to our CYO in that it comprises young men and women of high school age. My reception was cordial even though I was pinch hitting for a young confrere who at the eleventh hour found he could not be there. The teenage audience was not prepared for the Methuselah of white and fast-thinning hair who was introduced to them. The sight of me must, however, have has a sobering effect because squirming and the creaking of chairs were at the welcome minimum.

The subject suggested was "Catholic Symbols," the original plan having been to take the young people to the parish church and there to explain the furnishings and appurtenances of Catholic worship. I decided, therefore, to make a few general remarks by way of introduction to questions from the floor. This worked well, for the questions came thick and fast—and they were good ones.

Here are some samples: "Why are you called 'Father?'" Non-Catholics, unless they are Anglican or Orthodox, have trouble with this to us most natural address; these polite young people called me "Sir," the most courteous and respectful address they know. I did not mind because I understood them. "Why do you dress as you do?" I reminded them that the wearing of the clerical collar is more and more common among their own clergy nowadays. And from the *trivia* we went to more important matters: "Why do you pray in Latin? . . . Why do you confess to a priest? . . . What is the Mass? . . . Why are your services so elaborate?" I was here reminded of my own youth when these very questions plagued my curiosity. In those days one would not have invited a priest to answer them; one simply pondered them and continued in his ignorance. Can it be doubted that things are vastly improved in our time?

From the older members came the more mature questions. Our view, for example, of ecumenism and the importance of the Vatican Council; the Catholic view of mixed marriages; the status of the baptized Non-Catholic; why Catholics are forbidden to take part in non-Catholic rites—always difficult and nearly impossible to answer to their satisfaction; what hopes there are for advance toward the reunion of all Christians; why devotion to Mary is allowed, as they see it, to obscure the centrality of Christ; these and many others which testified to the alertness of these young men and women to the issues of the times. Again, I thought how extraordinary these youngsters are, for in my time we should not have has either the interest or the intelligence to raise such questions or to seek answers to them.

It was indeed a satisfactory meeting if only because the atmosphere was friendly and favorable to understanding. We parted at the door leading into the handsome old church. The meeting was to close there with a "worship service" led by the young people—an office consisting of psalms, Scripture, a hymn and prayers. I was invited to join them and perforce declined. (And here I go out on a limb.) I thought with sorrow of the great scandal of Christians being separated from one another. I thought, shall I live to see the day when, on occasions like these, we shall be able to pray together, when I can recite at least our Lord's own prayer with our separated brothers? Must we wait, I thought, until we are sitting together on the same heap of ashes to pray to our common Father through him whom in common we call Lord? My hosts wore bewilderment writ large on their young faces, as I turned away. My own heart at having to do so was heavy.

How Far is 'Too Far?'—March 11, 1966

If we have a quick answer to this one question, it may turn out to be the wrong one. "Wrong," that is, in that time may modify or revise it. Our ecumenical encounters have thus far—and we are only beginning—varied from the tentative to the bold and imaginative. Yet, how relative it all is: To one fearful of or hostile to ecumenism, the tentative venture appears to be "going too far," to one who has made the tentative venture, the more daring essays in this movement seem extreme and, again, are thought to be "carrying things too far." To the Lutheran of the Missouri Synod, any venture (even in the direction of his non-Missouri Lutheran brethren) is "going too far." To some Anglicans (as witness the picketing recently outside Westminster Abbey) any serious encounter with Catholics is "going too far." And one surmises that what happened the other day out in Missouri is to many a Catholic bishop in this country "going too far." But how far is "too far?" If one may credit the fragmentary reports from Holland of intercommunion and "interconcelebration," surely the limit has been surpassed; surely this is "going too far." Is it? I wonder how time will answer the questions.

Zealots, extremists, and imprudent men there will always be, I suppose, but time has a way of tempering these. (I am not denying that Christendom has had to pay a high price for some of them.) Yet, it is not from these men, I think, that any threat to sweet reasonableness can be expected today. I know nothing of the Hollanders whom one reads of, but from the accounts of the doings recently in our Midwest I have the impression that those gathered there, beginning with my old Anglican friend, Bishop Edward Welles, were without exception men of requisite learning, balanced purpose, and sound judgement. What is important, too, they had the backing and blessing of their respective superiors.

We are, most of us in this country, so new at this business of ecumenism that we have yet to get a true perspective. German, Dutch, French, and English Catholics and their Protestant confreres have been at it for generations. I recall Gregory Dix telling me how during World War II his (Anglican) Benedictine community of Nashdom shared alternately with the Benedictines of Downside each other's houses for the annual retreat. Each community celebrated its Eucharist successively each morning in the presence of the whole gathering. Both communities sang the Office in the common choir. This was 1940–1946! The result, well, what result would you expect? A tremendous affinity between the two communities. A compelling sense of Christian brotherhood. What is even more important, a real suffering together of the blessed "agony of separation." On the Continent, so Dix told me, he was always given a stall in choir in any Benedictine house he stayed at, and was provided with vessels, vestments, and altar for his daily Eucharist. The same reciprocity prevails at our own Mount Saviour as it does at the Anglican Benedictine house at Three Rivers, Michigan.

Thus, what went on last summer at Arlington, outside Boston is not as new and as daring and as "far out" as some thought it. My own view is that the times being never more urgent than they are today, the Holy Spirit is prodding us to move forward.

One of the great services our religious houses (some of them, that is) can perform today is just this: where there is zeal for the cause of Christian unity, where there is opportunity for serious and quiet study, where the requisite learning already exists, the sense of Christian brotherhood can be fostered under the best of possible conditions. Colloquia, retreats, times of recollection and recreation together, common prayer in choir, and (I would hope) "dual-eu-charistic" celebrations where Anglicans and Orthodox are present—these the authorities on both sides should encourage. There are not new and strange (and, therefore, possibly "dangerous") in Christendom today. There are simply novelties in what is really a provincial American Church. There! Out on a limb go I!

One more observation: Christian ecumenism is more than a "good feeling" between neighbors; it is more than being "buddy-buddy," it is more than the breezy use of first names; it is more that discovering that so-and-so down the street is "a great guy"—and a good golfer, too! Ecumenism involves pain: pain, because it means seeing Christ in your (Protestant or Catholic) brother, loving him in Christ, and for the time being suffering together within your separated condition.

Goodness, Poverty, Gospel—August 18, 1967

"Our eyes and ears convince us," wrote John Wesley, "there is not a less happy body of men in all England than the country farmer. There, life is supremely dull, usually unhappy, too." This remark provides the key to the vigor, the amazing spread, and the popularity of Methodism in 18th-century England and America. For the Church of England at the time was the church of lazy privilege, of sceptic rationalism, of a dark lost ignorance, and it had nothing to say to the middle-class poor and to the wretched masses of the people. Methodism was thus born out of apathy in the Establishment and out of loss of faith in the virtually moribund institution by those who eagerly embraced it. Wesley is properly said not so much to have left the Church of England as to have been disowned by it. His simple scriptural apostolate, his appeal to goodness and to the sources of grace: it was these that proved disturbing to the lazy, the privileged, and the comfortably off.

Methodism began as a movement within the Church of England. It was their regular, indeed weekly, attendance upon the Eucharist, in a period when Eucharistic celebrations in parish and collegiate churches were held only three or four times a year, that won for Charles Wesley and a small group of friends at Oxford the name of "Methodists." This was before John Wesley joined them there. Their living by rule and dependence upon the Sacrament—called forth the ridicule of their fellow students and the disapproval of the authorities. For any show of "enthusiasm" in matters of religion there was only deepest contempt.

John Wesley was born at the dawn of the century in a Lincolnshire rectory. He took holy orders and was for a time a fellow at Lincoln College in Oxford. In the early days of his ministry he had a high regard for the history, doctrine, and authority of the Church. But upon finding doors closed to him and the cold shoulder turned on him, he persuaded himself that he had attached too great importance to antiquity and to the Church councils. It was at this point that he took to ordaining his own men, for he claimed that he was "every bit as much an episcopos" as any bishop on the English bench; and if the English bishops refused him the pulpits of their parish churches and declined to ordain his candidates, then this was not to stand in the way of his movement.

Wesley was a man of tremendous energy and passion; he must have had a genius for organization; certainly of his eloquence there is abundant evidence. He is said to have suffered painfully in his early search for the "blessed assurance" of salvation. Hence, the watchword of Methodism was to become the "experience" of salvation through conversion of life—a deep conviction of sin, repentance, an acceptance of salvation through the merits and death of Christ, and then a direct call to the duty of "witnessing" and of preaching to others. Large bands of lay preachers and ordained "superintendents" travelled the length and breadth of Britain to win great numbers of the poor and the unchurched. The Methodist mission to Oglethorpe's colony of miserable outcasts in Georgia is the origin of the Methodist renewal in America.

The simple, usually ugly, frame church in the average American small town or village; the miserably paid parson; the generally "unfashionable" congregation; these are still the visible signs of the history and ethos of Methodism. It is not from snobbishness or a sense of superiority that I call attention to them. Rather, it is that I think them enviable and admirable signs; for they stand as a rebuke to much in organized Christianity as we know it that fails to speak of Christ to the world.

Are Conversions Declining—June 24, 1966

Two years ago this spring I wrote something in this place on this subject. Since then, ecumenical exchanges have vastly increased in numbers, in extent, and in the enlarging of understanding, mutual trust, and goodwill on both sides. The question is often raised, "What are we to do about conversions?" or, "Does all this mean that conversions will stop?" Urgent though the questions are, the answer to them is far from simple.

Doubtless you have seen in some of our popular periodicals letters from disturbed Catholics, all of them converts. "Why did I bother to become a Catholic?"—thus begins the typical query. Why, if, say the services are in English?—as though the vernacular were a step backward in the direction of Protestantism; or, why, if the structure of the Mass is to be made to conform to Reformation principles?- as though many of these allegedly "Reformation" principles were not in fact very sound liturgical canons; or, why, if the doctrine of papal infallibility is to be "watered down?"—the vulgar misunderstanding of "collegiately." These questions and others like them reflect a kind of resentment that the old order is changing and giving place to the new. Conversion, it seems to these writers, was not worth the candle. That their questions arise more from ignorance of the meaning of "renewal" than from knowledge does nothing to diminish their importance to those who ask them.

I know this because I have often asked myself this question: had Vatican II been projected and convened; had men like Father Weigel, Tavard, and Kung been writing and lecturing; had visits of state by non-Catholic ecclesiastics to Rome been as common as they are now; had Pope John been in Peter's chair, had all these "exchanges" been taking place—cardinals preaching and praying in Episcopal churches, Protestant clergyman appearing vested in Catholic sanctuaries: had these happened before my conversion, would I have made the step? I put this question to a young friend of mine, himself a priest and a convert. His answer was forthright to say the least, reflecting the courage as well as the foreshortened perspective of his twenty-odd years: "No," said he, "or very probably not."

As for me, all I can say is, I don't know. There is never a time when the claims of the Church to be herself—"the same yesterday, today, and always"—are not true and compelling; but their impact on those separated from her varies and has varied from time to time according to the accidents and circumstances of history. Whether today they would appear to me as urgent as they appeared then, I simply cannot say.

What I do know is that my friends on the other side of the ecumenical fence are more confirmed than even in the tenability of their position today—and this despite, or perhaps because of, their growing trust in and respect for the Church's efforts toward her own renewal and, therefore, toward the unity of all Christians. I suspect, too, that "Roman fever" is far less frequent even among the most advanced (that is, pro-Papal) Anglicans than it was a decade ago. Moreover, according to the rules agreed upon by all participants, the dialogue between ourselves and non-Catholics precludes either a defense of the several claims of the participants to be right of any attempt by either side to win over the other to its position. Controversy is frowned upon. Forbearance is the means and growing understanding is the end of dialogue. This vastly changed and daily changing atmosphere cannot, it seems to me, but have the effect of reducing the number of conversions to the Roman Church, at least among the intelligent and widely read.

How this alters the manner of our "approaches" to non-Catholic in good faith, what its effect will be on the efforts of pastors and missionaries to win converts: these are questions that only time will answer. And where, meanwhile, is the line to be drawn between leaving the non-Catholic in good faith and persuading him that he does not yet enjoy that fullness of life and grace which is found only in the one Church of Christ? The answer is, I think, not as simple today as it seemed only a little while ago.

And how, with all that is happening, are we to view the person who, in good faith, leaves the Catholic Church to become, say, an Orthodox or an Anglican? There are such. The answer to this is no longer quite simple. If indeed it ever was.

May it be that God has his own way of gathering his people into unity? May it be, in his mysterious Providence, that all men must first work out their own self-renewal where they are? Or, is it possible that the stemming of the tide Romeward is only temporary? That once the Church displays her treasures new and old in all their splendor, men will see her for what she is and seek her in perhaps greater numbers than we can imagine? I like to think that this last is the vital question. And if it is, then let us get on apace with our own renewal.

Pastor of St. Francis of Assisi Church, South Windsor, Connecticut, 1963–1971

4

Liturgy

Tradition and Acculturation

THE CONSUMMATE RELIGIOUS IMPORTANCE of the liturgy was Gordon's frequent theme, for this was how the great church expressed itself; he based his presentations on the biblical theme of "gathering," and the old English word "ingathering." Christians across the ages have gathered, come together in a long term pilgrimage with Christ to the Father, and at the center of this pilgrimage is the Eucharist. As he studied the liturgical reforms in Rome, he contrasted ceremonial rigidity with the qualities of the Mass facing the people with its plain gestures and direct and simple Eucharistic prayer. Worship was active engagement of body, mind, and spirit, actualized by gestures and posture, attentive hearing, and interior change. For all that, he sympathized with those—often dear friends or parishioners—who felt that it was just such active participation that prevented them from praying! He told them that silent, personal prayer, though essential, might also be the enemy of deeply engaged participation. Other enemies to active, participatory prayer would be superfluous ceremonial in the sanctuary and tasteless music for the congregation.

For Gordon, the home Eucharist was the archetypal Eucharist, closest to the Last Supper, valid for all intimate gatherings. Families could surround a central table, use décor appropriate to a home meal setting, bake the breads, and discuss biblical themes together. He praised exuberant small school gatherings with foremass and homily out in nature and Eucharist in a small chapel with students gathered around the altar and receiving both the bread and the wine. Gordon's experience as rector of the Episcopal Church of the Resurrection in New York City animated his love of liturgical beauty. Although he rejoiced to recall the prayers and movements in his superbly set-up sanctuary at Resurrection, he thought that even that could not serve as the standard model for the liturgies he envisioned for the future. Yet, when contemporary ways had gone awry, as in the care of the dead, he allowed himself to draw on the past, proposing a vigil in the home and the office of the dead in the church chantry.

Proposals for liturgical celebrations in churches, chapels, and in the home were clear and to the point: words, sounds, and space were the key features to be attended to. Accordingly, many columns praised and criticized liturgical translations—but not without praising the joys of the Latin Mass at Notre Dame Cathedral and in one or two American churches, where congregants lustily jointed in the singing. He hoped that these values could be perpetuated in collegiate and monastic churches. He praised as beautiful Eucharistic celebrations, the historical texts of the Anglican Church, such as the First Prayer Book of Edward VI, the Scottish Prayer Book, and the American Episcopal liturgy. These provided direct and simple formulas with emphasis on the invocation of the Holy Spirit upon the gifts and the words of institution. Gordon had no patience then, with Catholic priests, both old and young, who raced through prayers, reducing them to near gibberish, because this was irreverence toward God, a stain on the image of the Church, and damaging to the apostolate.

Some columns praised or lamented church architecture, coming out squarely for simplicity of design but also for richness of preaching, presiding, and vesture inside the church. In earlier centuries, church art and décor served a teaching function, but today plainness, austerity, and "emptiness" of the building should place in relief the altar of sacrifice, the place of reservation, the lectern for readings, and the baptismal font. Emptiness is thus filled with Holy Presence. In a more casual mode, he recommended a book on the new churches of Europe, sixty of them, with the German churches overall the best. The photos and texts made it clear that Europe was far ahead of America, where the responsible clergy often mistrusted any innovation. In Europe, although there was no single model layout, the effort to keep the people close to the altar, the placement of the entrances, the distribution of light, and the seating (no pews), all hastened and strengthened the liturgical renewal.

A combination of technical originality and pastoral ingenuity could provide music for the new English liturgical texts. For example, some earlier Anglican attempts would be worth attending to, as well as the current efforts at the American Benedictine monastery of Mount Saviour to do the old Latin chants in English. Gordon knows from experience that plain chant does submit to adaptation, because his church choir of adults and youths already does it, and he knows that he will eventually have the whole congregation joining in.

Gordon wrote up his trips and stop-offs to visit new churches, praising in particular St. Mark's Episcopal Church in New Canaan, Connecticut, a building of gothic design with modern materials. With a high altar and long sanctuary, a rich reredos portraying the drama of redemption, the stained glass themes of nativity, eucharist, and resurrection. He reports his soul-enriching visits in earlier years to the Paulist, the Jesuit, and the Corpus Christi churches of New York City, where he could hear the great Catholic preachers Bede Jarrett, William Orchard, and George Ford. Worship and preaching were no better than in the best of the Episcopal churches he knew, but they rang uniquely true.

On 'Gathering' God's People—October 22, 1965

Recently in Goshen, the village of my birth, the Congregationalists observed the 225th anniversary of the founding of their church. In 1740, so runs the account, the Church of Christ Congregational, its official title, was "gathered." The word so intrigued me that I looked it up in the Oxford Dictionary, supposing it to be of Old English, and therefore of pre-Reformation origin. Sure enough, I found "gather" to mean "to congregate, assemble, OE." This, then, thought I, must account for a word much nowadays in writings on liturgy to refer to coming together of the people for divine worship, the word "ingathering." Is there such a word I asked; or has it been coined? There is: and it was in use at least as early as 1535. It means "the action of gathering in" and refers especially to autumn harvest.

Whence, for the Orthodox Jew, the "Feast of the Ingathering," or the nine-day harvest festival known by its Hebrew name, *Sukkoth*. Incidentally, this is also the Feast of the Tabernacles ("tabernacles" means, simply, "little tent") during which the ancient people of God live in small green arbors or tents—in other words, they camped out—to remind themselves of their passage through the wilderness on their way to the Land of Promise.

Two ideas emerge from this: the bountiful harvest and the people's desire to return thanks to God: and their awareness that they were but pilgrims and travelers through this world. These are two profoundly *eucharistic* ideas. It is wonderful what tracking down a seemingly obvious word will uncover!

And so, to the business of this essay, which has to do with churchgoing. Ask the (I fear, typical) layman why he comes to church on the Lord's Day. He comes, he will tell you, to carry out the first precept, ("You gotta go to church, don't you?"). The penalty for failure, he will add, is mortal sin. Much as I respect obedience, and necessary as it is, I submit that we should do something to correct this minimal behavior. That it will take some doing I am the first to allow.

What is the meaning of our attendance at Mass on Sundays and other feasts? First of all, our coming together is a journey, a pilgrimage, as is our entire course through this life. And our journey begins when, on our Lord's own day—it is *his* day, not ours!—we get up and leave our homes. Whether we walk a mere step or drive a great distance, the act of worshipping God begins with our trip to church. Why? Because we are on our way to "gather" the Church together in one place, to leave one world in order to enter another, and a new world: to forsake one life in order to enter a new—and our true—life. Our worship, then, begins not when we arrive at church, but rather in the act of setting out; for at that point in home after home, begins the "ingathering" of the people of God. If we fail to go at all, the "ingathering" will be incomplete; the body of the faithful will be deprived of its full membership, will be the poorer and the weaker because we are not there.

Thus, my motive is transformed: I get up, start out, and come to church because I am needed to make the holy assembly complete. A pilgrim am I on my way to that "better country"—to that foretaste of my true country, which God has promised me and to which he will one day admit me. If I have such thoughts as these in mind—and I can, and should, think them as I get ready for church, and I should share them with my family—will I not set out in good time, prayerfully conscious of what my family and I are about, and about to be, and about to do?

But I go to Mass (the Eucharistic Sacrifice and Meal, the great Thanksgiving) for another reason. I join the "ingathering" of God's people in order, together with them, to return thanks through Christ to my heavenly Father. For what, I ask myself as I set out with my family from my home, what do I have that I have not received from him?

A traveler, then, through this world, whose heart is thankful: this is the Catholic Christian on his way to Mass. Compare this with, "You gotta go to Mass, don't you?"

Changed by the 'Changes'—June 3, 1965

We hear more these days about the "changes" in the Mass than about the *change* in the lives of Catholics. The "changes" are and will be of trifling consequences unless there is, as a result of them, a great *change* in us all. The "changes" are only in matters external. Externals change from age to age, from century to century, and may do so again and perhaps often in our lifetime. But they themselves do not in any way change the doctrine, discipline, or worship of the Church; they do not alter the essential order and structure of the Catholic and Christian life. The Church remains "the same yesterday, today, and always." What must change, then, is ourselves. What must affect us all, and deeply, is the meaning underlying the "changes." And the meaning is, quite simply, a renewal—a making new again.

The making new again is three-fold: it is to be a continual refreshment of the body, mind, and spirit—a renewal, that is of the whole man. We have no trouble accepting the notion and the fact of the soul's refreshment, for there has been no want of teaching on this aspect of worship and of sacramental growth. What is certainly new to most of us is the notion that the new ways of worship work a renewing of mind and of body. This, surely, is obvious to those who had had years of training in the liturgical life; it is beginning to be appreciated by the few who have this half-year past taken kindly and given themselves heart and soul to the new order.

That there is opportunity for daily renewal of the mind is certain. Hearing the Word of God as the readings vary from day to day; hearing it explained and applied, even briefly, every morning in the homily: how can this do otherwise than enrich our knowledge of God, of his love, of his will for us, of ourselves? But even so, we must *listen* and we must *hear*. Only a mind really alert can become daily more alert. "He who has ears to hear, let him hear." It is possible to "hear" and yet not really *hear*. Listening attentively, and really hearing: this is as much prayer as what we have taken prayer to be.

But a renewal of the body? How can this be? It is because we in this country are now learning what European Catholics have long known—that standing is the characteristically Christian posture of worship, especially of praise and not infrequently of adoration itself. In how many Roman churches, for example, there are no pews, no kneeling benches! Except for the consecration, Europeans stand throughout Canon. In many churches the worshipers stand to receive Communion. Too long in America have we been a kneeling, breast-beating body of worshippers. We have too long been taught that kneeling is the only proper posture for prayer; too long have we been allowed to reoccupy our minds and prayer with our unworthiness rather than be overwhelmed with the joy of our calling as the sons of God and brothers of Christ. And we have not raised our voices in songs of praise practically since the beginnings of the Church in this country. Small wonder is it that we are shocked by the almost carnival atmosphere of worship abroad and in the Oriental churches! But all this is changing and the change, believe it or not, is being worked by simply making attendance at Mass and exercise of the body, and an active exercise at that. We are being made to work and the physical exertion will in time sharpen our minds and alert our senses, as exercise is meant to do, and does, in the physical order.

The commonest objection one hears to all this is that it is "distracting." Distracting? Well, that depends on what you have been accustomed to doing. It is admittedly a distraction from private devotion; it is destructive of the stillness of the heart's communion with God. But the Mass is public action, not private prayer. The Mass is public work, a busy activity, and not passive repose. I think that of all that we have to learn, and re-learn, this is perhaps the first and hardest lesson of all. And for those who find it hard to learn I, for one, have abundant sympathy, not because I share their discomfort but because I read in their faces the irritation and the will to resist. Yet it will be seen a year from today to be easier than it is now, and easier five years from now; and let a decade go by, and we shall wonder how we ever found the former ways satisfying. We shall have been changed by the "changes"—and immeasurably for the better.

Our Worship is an Action—October 29, 1964

The questioner is a friend of mine in his sixties, Jesuit-trained in his youth at the English Stonyhurst College, who has rarely missed daily Mass all his adult life. "Father," he asked the other day, "will you explain to me why Low Mass is no longer quiet and prayerful, why our devotions are constantly being interrupted, why there must be all this distraction—this talking and standing and sitting at unaccustomed times and places throughout Mass? For me the Mass is being spoiled. I find it impossible any longer to pray."

And the question is one we shall have to answer in season and out of season. It is Monsignor Guardini, I believe, who quotes the old pastor as saying in his bewilderment with the changing order of things, "There was a time when my people could pray at Mass. Now all they do is talk and get up and down." One would have to be singularly without feeling not to have much sympathy for him. This, then, is the difficulty for hosts of devout Catholics: the Mass as an occasion for quiet personal devotion and meditation, or the Mass as being primarily a public action, a liturgy, which by definition is the people's work at worship.

My friend, for example, as far as I can observe, never adopted the hitherto widespread use of the people's missal—and what is more out of date today than the laymen's missal! We are directed to "sit and listen" to the epistle, to "stand and hear" the gospel, not to follow along with the reading, because an attentive listening is a more direct encounter with the Word of God than a private reading or following of the text. My friend's book of devotion, on which was raised from childhood, is the classic, 17th-century anthology of prayers, Bishop Challoner's *Garden of the Soul*. The very title suggests both the outlook and the behavior of the passive, non-participating worshiper. Mind you, there is no calling into question here the dispositions, the sincerity, the whole-hearted self-giving at Mass of such persons as my friend. Yet, what we must do for him is to wean him away from long and steady habits of private devotion and commend what is surely the better way. We must urge him to forsake his place at the back of the church ("where," he says, "I can be quiet and say my prayers") and to move up to the center of the liturgical activity, as near to the altar as possible where he becomes a *circumstans*, one who "stands close" to the place of sacrifice.

What we do for him, then, is to broaden his understanding of prayer, for up to this time he has thought of prayer as being personal and private, an interior disposition rather than in any sense or at specified times and external act. It is not an exaggeration to say that of prayer in common, of public worship, he knows next to nothing. True, he would not be silent at public Rosary or at the Stations of the Cross or during the "prayers after Mass," but at Mass, where of all places and times his voice should be heard, is still. He has not been taught all these years that public worship must engage the whole man—his body and mind as well as his spirit: that public worship makes its rightful demand on his body: "let us stand . . . and sit . . .

kneel," even *walk* from place to place while singing the Offertory or Communion hymns; that it summons his mind to hear and make his own the lessons of the day, and of every day; that it requires his voice in praise, in petition, and it loud assent. *And all this activity is prayer!* It is this that he does not realize.

It is prayer of a most necessary, most special kind—liturgical prayer, the active prayer and the prayerful activity of the people of God "at work at worship." Thus, the posture of the body at Mass can be, is in fact, an act of prayer. The voice vigorously used in praise and response is and instrument of prayer. This carrying of the bread and wine to the altar: this, too, is prayer. The communion procession accompanied by song is prayer.

And what is more, it is the best possible prayer my friend can engage in when he meets with the faithful for the sacrifice-meal. For he with all the faithful makes up the Church. Christ's living body, Christ's worshipping body. A living body is not inactive unless it is paralyzed. But the body of Christ is alive and strong, and never more so than when it is at worship. Therefore, it acts, and its action is the prayer supreme.

You Mean What You Say—October 13, 1967

A priest asked me the other day, "Do you really believe the things you write?" And seeing my astonishment, he quickly added, "Or do you write sometimes simply to stir up the animals?" By nature a man of peace, I let sleeping dogs lie; yet I told my friend that I mean what I say and try to say what I mean.

Not always, however, have I believed some of the things I have lately come to believe. For example, I once as an Anglican defended the propers of the Mass, especially when these were sung. It was experience with them and with their effect on the people (the effect being supreme boredom) that convinced me of their irrelevance to parish worship. (Did you, by the way, relish last Sunday's Offertory—all about poor Job and his boils? Or the Offertory of the week before—about weeping beside Babylon's waters?) And I can remember making in the old days a very good case for the nine-fold Kyries, and for the Gloria at the beginning rather than, according to Anglican usage, at the end of the rite. I can recall, not so long ago, hearing my young friend, Father [Charles] Riepe, one of the country's most competent liturgical scholars, urge radical surgery for our Roman rite, and at the dinner table taking vehement issue with him. So I have come round, perhaps "grown," to a point of view about these things that I have not always held. Why?

Because, I think, we are learning to forsake form for content and meaning. Anglicans, especially the old-fashioned "High" variety, love form and ceremony. And I look back on the days when to my mind there was nothing in this world more sublime than Solemn Mass with great music and full Roman ceremonial. I taught my people to love this with a passion. We burned more incense, believe it or not, on one Sunday morning than I use now in a year! The "house," like the temple in Isaiah's vision, "was filled with smoke." Now, I do not care if I never witness or take part again in a solemn function. Why? Because I have come to know something infinitely more compelling, more moving, more satisfying, more effective.

For all the majesty and splendor of worship as I once knew I wouldn't trade what goes on Sunday by Sunday in my parish church. True, we have two sung Masses a Sunday, and beautifully sung they are; but they are simple, and quite free of studied formality. We "sit loose," so to say, and in the sanctuary our attitudes and behavior are natural. No more holding the hands just so; no more degrees of bows, slight, medium, and deep; no pious posturing of any sort. What a relief!

Three changes, I think, account for this: the turning-about of the altar—for what we used to do with our backs to people now is manifestly absurd when we face them; the simplification of the celebrant's and ministers' movements—for this makes for doing only those things that mean something, of that get something needful done. And, finally, the new English Canon for this splendid prayer says what it means and means what it says in the briefest compass, and all redundancies and duplications and tiresome verbiage are a thing of the past. Praise be!

Table at Home, Church—January 3, 1969

Nothing so far in my experience is so persuasive of the close relationship between the family board, presided over by the father and priest of his household, and the altar than is the occasion of the home Eucharist. Nothing, too, more clearly demonstrates that the Mass is essentially a meal than does the home Eucharist. For what this experience is worth I should like to share it with my readers.

We were at pains last spring to tell our people that requests for Mass in the home should properly come from them and that in general the motive should be the desire of a neighborhood to express its Christian unity or of parishioners to express a common interest or work in the life of the parish. Accordingly, the first request came from the members of the adult choir early in the summer. Later a home Eucharist was celebrated for the executive board and the workers in the parish Confraternity of Christian Doctrine. Husbands, wives, and children were invited to share the experience.

One of the most rewarding occasions was a family reunion: a new house was blessed: the engagement of the elder son was celebrated: and the return from across the country of the daughter and her soldier husband with the new grandchild was hailed by the numerous relatives of the family who gathered from far and near. That Christ should on those occasions be both host and guest and food was an experience none there will soon or easily forget.

As to the procedure at these home Eucharists my own feeling is that everything should suggest home and nothing should suggest church. The table should be laid with the housewife's choice of linen, her own candelabrum, flowers if desired, and these should be the setting for the Eucharistic cup and plate. I have in mind, too, a magnificent tavern table in a Colonial kitchen facing a great fireplace and oven: these I would leave quite plain and unadorned—as they are when the family sits down to a meal.

The bread might appropriately be of the housewife's own baking. (On one occasion we used an imported Syrian bread not unlike, I think, what our Lord used at his home Eucharist). I see no point at all in bringing along the customary altar paraphernalia—altar cards, cross, missal, and the like—such as appeared in a recent news photograph of a home Mass in New York. This to me is bringing the Church to the home; my point is that our procedure demonstrates that the family and its home are, as St. Chrysostom said, "a little church."

Also, in my view, Eucharistic vestments at home are about as appropriate as top hat, white tie, and tails at a cookout. You can see that I am impatient with the framers of the average set of diocesan guidelines for insisting on a churchly procedure and for failing to leave a wide margin for the informality and improvisation. The prayers need not—in fact, should not—be those of a given "Mass of the day." Rather, they should be carefully prepared and then quite informally offered to accord with the interests of the assembly.

This principle, too, should govern the choice of readings, if any, I say "if any" because the best fore-Mass would be a discursive one, especially if the assembly is capable of sustaining a conversation with the leader and among themselves, for, say, 10 or 12 minutes. The prayer of the faithful should be quite free and spontaneous. And for the sake of brevity and clarity we have used the new Eucharistic Prayer I—the so-called Canon of Hippolytus, the oldest if not indeed the first Canon in the Church's treasury of prayers. The occasion of a home Eucharist is also the ideal situation for the receiving of the Eucharist under both species.

These are my impressions based on what I regard as a precious experience. But more telling by far is the effect the home Eucharist has on the participants. It is not difficult to tell when human beings are profoundly moved. One person said to me, "I see now what you mean when you talk about the Lord's 'banquet table.' I shall appreciate the holy meal in church now more than ever before." The point, I felt, had been well taken.

One Kind of 'Experiment'—September 8, 1967

Prey to the mild fear of crowds, I have all my adult life avoided large gatherings, when in conscience I could do so. Hence, I rarely go to conventions, populous meetings or conferences, and so have never attended the annual liturgical conference. What I glean of what is going on, I get by word of mouth or, mostly, by reading. "Experimental liturgy" is one of the aspects of renewal with which I am currently least acquainted.

Imagine, then, my good fortune when, on a sparkling day last week, my Anglo-American friends and I drove to Lenox to see the Gengras memorial chapel at Cranwell School. Incidentally, as I have noted earlier in this place, the chapel is an absolute knock-out and should be seen. There is only one (and that, I think, a glaring) fault: I mean the hanging Rood over the altar. I leave you to judge for yourself, since criticism of the building and the appointments is not here our concern.

We arrived as the noon Angelus was ringing. Behind the chapel, overlooking a magnificent valley and either Greylock or Ascutney in the distance, a group of perhaps half a hundred boys was seated on the ground. A priest was addressing them. What this exercise was we did not know, and made our way into the church.

Mass had either just been celebrated, or was about to be, for the candles were lighted and the appointments in evidence. The answer was forthcoming, for presently the boys entered. They came in most informally, and were in very casual dress—suntans, shorts, athletic jerseys, and what have you. I could read astonishment in John's face, he having been English-Jesuit-trained at Stonyhurst half a century ago.

To a stirring folk hymn, gloriously sung, led by three guitars, the celebrant and concelebrants entered. Straightaway the boys made their offering of bread, forming a procession round about the altar. (This led me to surmise that the fore-Mass and homily had been given out on the hillside.)

The celebrant appeared to improvise a prayer over the offerings in the simplest and most direct of language. This was also true of the preface. Though read from a sheet of paper, the canon, too, was a short and direct statement: viz, we bless God for his work of creation, for our life and work, and supremely for sending us his Son; "who, on the night before he suffered, took bread," etc.: what followed upon this simple Consecration was similarly brief and simple, thoroughly understandable because there was not a syllable of conventional liturgical idiom.

Communion was given to all in both kinds, the boys forming two lines to receive the Host and then proceeding, one line to each end of the Table, to receive from the Cup in their own hands. Mass ended with a short, again improvised, statement of thanksgiving.

This experience was so completely and genuinely sense-making, so evidently meaningful for all, that I long for the day when the parish Eucharist can be celebrated in this manner on weekdays and on other special occasions. I should think it could be done tomorrow in small churches.

On the Care of the Dead—November 14, 1963

The title is not mine. It is St. Augustine's for his classic treatise on this Christian and corporal work of mercy. What he says bears reading at any time, but especially today when much on this matter is being written and discussed. Of particular interest, it seems to me, is his insistence on simplicity and directness: the direct confronting of death with faithful prayer; the simple committing of the body, without fuss or ado, to the good earth from whence it came.

For what they are worth, the following are my reflections on the care of the dead in our time. I suppose that during those years in New York undertakers regarded me as one of the meddlesome clergy, for on certain Christian usages long-hallowed I would insist and of certain new-fangled and to me quite barbaric customs I would have none in my church. This was not always easy, but remaining firm made in the end for decent Christian burial. This is what I insisted upon at a time when the campaign to cover up and disguise death beneath lush, really quite inadmissible, floral displays and other forms of sentimental claptrap were getting the upper hand.

The first thing I insisted on was the use of the funeral pall over the coffin. My church owned one of the most handsome palls I have ever seen. Handmade in England, woven of black silk shot through the gold thread, and bearing an embroidered medallion of the Risen Christ, it not only proclaimed that there is no distinction in death between high and low, rich and poor; it also struck for the onlooker the double note of sorrow and of triumph. It was a useful device as well as an eloquent symbol. As soon as my present parish can afford it, I am going to have a funeral pall. As long as I am here, it will be used without exception—perhaps, at my end, for me!

Rarely in New York 20 years ago did the question where to lay out the dead arise. Mortuary chapels-so-called were still a novelty; besides, my people were conservative enough to opt for the customs of their parents. Thus, the dead were kept at home until the time for the funeral in church. On this practice it is hard. I think, to improve; but I suppose that there are circumstances nowadays that dictate the use of the mortuary.

That I heartily dislike the prevailing custom is of no importance except to me, but strongly about it do I indeed feel. If I could, I would always encourage the bereaved to have their dead with them at home. I would urge them to make of the "calling hours" as little of a social occasion as is consonant with friendliness and courtesy. I do not like what I see of the typical "wake." And the typical mortuary I find depressing, cheerless, anything but "homelike."

By far the best procedure, and we adopted it whenever it was possible to do so, was to bring the body to the church the day before the funeral. If ever I were to build a church (a prospect highly unlikely) I should build a crypt chapel, a "chantry" as it was called in the old, old days—a chapel where the dead were brought and where the Liturgy of the Dead was performed.

We had no chantry in New York, but we improvised one in a side vestibule. Here we gathered the family and friends about the coffin (closed!) and recited the psalms and read the lessons of the Church's liturgy. We used the Office of the Dead in translation and a more fortifying, a nobler, a more consoling spiritual exercise for the Christian mourner it would indeed be hard to find. Admittedly—and alas!—this amounts in our time to a special culture. But it is one I should like to see encouraged among those of our people who are ready for it. There must be some who would welcome it.

The Horns of the Dilemma—June 1, 1961

Don't mistake me: I love the Latin of the liturgy. I first came to know it in part by hearing the great masses of Haydn, Mozart, and Beethoven. (I did not know then how wholly unsuitable is the music of these works for common worship.) Here, I sensed, was a language unequalled for its sonorous majesty, its restraint, its beauty. Later, hearing the chant, it seemed to me that the vernacular, like the English now used in some operas, was a pale thing indeed alongside the original.

I recall a Sunday in June 1934—"the last time I saw Paris"—when my mother and I assisted at Mass in Notre Dame. The occasion was Youth Sunday. The great church was filled with young men and women from the metropolitan parishes. We sat in bleacher-like seats set up in the transepts. The cardinal (was it Verdier?) sang Mass facing the people at the altar in the crossing, his throne being at the opposite end of the choir. What I shall never forget is the congregational singing of the ordinary of the Mass. If anything could shake the vaulting of that noble church, it was the singing of those thousands.

I don't think that I am captive to any "mystique" associated with church Latin. Perhaps its hold on me derives from its strangeness to me. Even now, after twelve years in the Church, it is novel and unfailingly impressive. You who have nothing else may not share in my delight in it. Being as objective as I can be, my view is that here is a priceless culture, an inspired art form not lightly to be tossed aside. I cannot accustom myself to the thought that it will ever be given up in collegiate and monastic churches, or that it should be.

Two Sundays ago, I heard a congregation of three to four hundred sing the ordinary of the Mass. They did it beautifully, showing that they knew not only what they were about but what they were saying as they sang. I have seen and heard the same thing in Holy Cross parish, St. Louis, where years of education brought the shared liturgy to a nearly perfect thing. "It can be done," as they say, and it seems worth doing.

And yet, here is my problem. It may be a problem to hosts of us. We to whom Latin is at least a semi-living tongue, a second language in which we are more or less at our ease, are still an *elite*—a minority much enriched by our grasp of this classic culture, but a minority nevertheless. Meanwhile the exigencies of the times seem to demand the sacrifice of aesthetic for practical values. The vernacular is desperately needed in the missions of the Church. It is essential, I think, to the work of reunion. And the pastoral liturgy can never be directly furthered short of its wider use.

Has no one thought of a way to preserve both of these, the cultural and the practical? As for me, I have both hands firmly fixed on the two horns of the dilemma.

A Look into the Future—November 17, 1967

The first attempt to compose a Canon in English was made in 1549, at which time appeared the First Prayer Book of Edward VI. In many ways it is a glorious composition, a bit wordy in our view today, but nonetheless, and especially structurally, faithful to the pattern of splendid eucharistic prayers. Its counterpart, in use today, is found in the Scottish (Episcopal) Prayer Book. Both prayers are worth investigating. For the essay at hand I consider two notable features: the manner of dealing with the saints, and the presence of an invocation of the Holy Spirit on the offerings.

First, the saints. Instead of the familiar lists of names, in the 1549 book we read (and here, as best I can, I put the text in contemporary English): ". . . we give you praise and thanksgiving for the wonderful grace and virtue shown in all your saints from the beginning of the world: chiefly in the glorious and most blessed Virgin, mother of your Son, Jesus Christ, our Lord and God, and in the holy Patriarchs, Prophets, Apostles, and Martyrs, whose examples, faith and keeping your holy commandments, grant us to follow." There is no reference, you will note, to the prayers of the saints for us.

This is followed at once by a commemoration of "those who have died:" "We entrust to your mercy all your other servants who have departed from this world with the sign of faith, and who are now at rest: grant them your mercy and everlasting peace."

Both of these commemorations were dropped in the drastic revision of 1552, in Edward's Second Prayer Book, and were recovered for Anglican use in the Scottish book where, as we said, they appear today. From this source they found their way, in a greatly modified form, to the book used in the American Episcopal Church.

Directly before the words of institution in Edward's 1549 book occurs this beautiful invocation of the Holy Spirit: "Hear us, merciful Father, and with your Holy Spirit and Word, bless and sanctify these your gifts to us of bread and wine, that they may be for us the body and blood of your most dear Son, Jesus Christ. Who in the same night he was betrayed, took bread, and when he had given thanks," etc.

I have a friend in high place in the councils of liturgists, who, I am sure, would welcome our present Canon the omission of all references to the saints and the departed. He believes that these, coming late into our Eucharistic prayer, are more properly, as they were originally, the subject of the intercessory Prayer of the Faithful. Here, too, according to him, belong also the prayers for the whole Church—pope, bishops, clergy, and people.

Thus, were the early structure to be recovered in our day, the Canon of the Mass would be brief indeed and to the point. It would continue "this spirit of thanksgiving" following the opening dialogue of the preface: there would be an invoking of the Spirit on the offerings, followed by an account of the Last Supper; the anamnesis, or recalling the life, passion, death, resurrection, and ascension of Christ, would be made; and then the great doxology.

Is this the shape of the future for us? I should welcome it. In any event, there is no reason why, with all that is known today about the history of eucharistic prayers, we should not in the next ten years come up with an incomparable, indeed the best, Canon conceivable.

Does Haste Breed Contempt?—August 22, 1963

In a recent issue of *Time*, in an otherwise dull "cover story" on the Anglican Communion, mention was made of the stately prose of the Book of Common Prayer, and especially of its translations of the ancient collects. These, adds *Time*, are "one of man's finest efforts to address his Creator reverently." This observation recalled to me the years and years of churchgoing when, among many other good things, the sheer beauty of language and the care and skill with which it was read afforded an undeniable grace—one whose absence I have much mourned in the years that have passed.

Some weeks ago, on his return from retreat, my esteemed editor had much to say about the glories of the Divine Office and the Conventual Mass at St. Joseph's Abbey. How many of us, I wonder, took the time and trouble to read him carefully? By deft indirection he said something important to all of us, for in pointing to the merits of Mass well said and sung, he succeeded in identifying the faults, all too prevalent among us, that mar public worship in parish after parish. He chose the *via eminentissima*, the argument from excellence, and it is the softer, gentler persuasion.

But most priests, if they are like me, need a jolt from time to time. (I have revised this copy no fewer than four times to avoid giving offense to my peers and my betters). I have, believe me, no one in particular in mind, no one place, no one diocese. I do have in mind a condition that has plagued me these many years, one that strikes me as general in my few travels in this country.) There are many, many exceptions: younger priests especially, who give evidence of careful training, constant advertence, in the conduct of public worship; older priests by the scores who are a joy to listen to at the altar and from the pulpit and whose Mass is a work of studied grace. Yet the exceptions only show up the common deficiencies.

Why, I have wondered for years, do so many of us treat the texts and the ordered prayers of Catholic worship with so little apparent regard for their content? Why do we read them so badly? Why is our Latin often so void of expression, of pause and emphasis and regard for quantity, as to be unintelligible to the hearer? Why do we read it or sing it so rapidly? Is there some virtue in sheer haste? Why are the altar boys, once so carefully trained to make their answers intelligibly, so soon put off by us? Why do they lapse into our bad habits and in the end settle for a kind of professional gibberish that makes a mockery of canonized prayer?

Why the hurry? Our editor, you may recall, point out that nothing should mar the order and dignity of the parish Mass—not announcements, not even sermons, for the former can be printed and the latter better planned in the interest of brevity. Why, then, the hurry? Why this mad pursuit? Why should our Mass look to the observer like a mere chore to be got through as quickly as possible? Why—worst of all—should we give the impression of being ourselves supremely bored by it all? Our first Mass was not like this. What happened in the meantime?

And the English prayers! Why do we read them in a manner mechanical, unreflective, expressionless, cold, and curt! It would be well if we could hear ourselves as others hear us.

Our poor habits have bred contempt for the power and beauty of words. We have paid so little mind to what, out of habit day by day, we read as to deprive ourselves and our people of the grace of the word well spoken. And in this instance it is the *lectio divina*, the very Word of God!

The effects, it seems to me, are serious. They constitute a deterrent to the liturgy shared by the priests and people. They are an offense to many a sensitive lay ear. They are a material, if not a formal, irreverence before God to whom we are speaking. And in a time when the "image" of the Church was never better nor more respected by the outsider, they are a stain on that image; they mar a countenance otherwise fair and glorious. It is the countenance of the very Spouse of Christ, his dear Body, the Church.

The Filling of Emptiness—April 21, 1967

There is about the modern church building a quality of emptiness. This the average Catholic Christian finds hard to accept. We must try to help him.

Wherever there are priest and people, bread and wine, plate and cup, and an altar-table, there is the Church at worship. The place may be a catacomb or a battlefield; it may be Yankee Stadium; it may be the kitchen or the sick-room in someone's house. Or, what is more common, it may be what we call a church—a place set apart, more or less permanent, where a roof is supported by walls has been built to shelter the altar. Here in any given community the Church is gathered for worship.

When, in the west, about 1100 A.D., men began to decorate churches, they did so primarily to provide visual instruction for the people, books being uncommon at best and the people generally unable to read. Even so, medieval churches, though highly colorful, were really quite plain, even at their best, austere. It was with the Renaissance, four centuries later, that men went all out, in their often misguided genius, to fill their churches with "religious art" so-called. From this effort it was a short step indeed to the excesses which in succeeding centuries led to the bad taste and general clutter that the contemporary liturgical revival seeks to get rid of. Everywhere we are, or should be, cleaning house.

There is something about a bare wall that sets most of us itching to fill it. For some reason we are uncomfortable with sheer wall space. I am suggesting that there is more meaning, more strength, and in the end greater majesty and beauty in the "emptiness" of the austere church building that can be found in those buildings that mirror other and earlier times.

Four things are needed in a church, and only four: the Altar of Sacrifice, the place of Reservation for the Eucharistic presence, the Ambo for the proclaiming of the Word of God, and the Font. However these are placed matters perhaps little, except that they must be seen to be interdependent and yet each in its order to perform by sign and by function its role in the setting forth of the whole gospel of Christ. Whatever else is added must be subordinate lest it become a source of distraction.

A friend, back from her first trip to Europe, speaking of the Roman churches and the baroque churches in Austria, remarked, "But, Father, they are a feast for the eye!" That, it seems to me, is just the point: a feast for the eye. True, we feast our eyes on a multiplicity of objects, but what becomes of the real prayer? How can we be "lost in wonder, love, and praise?" Thus, the "emptiness" of our new churches is deliberate. These buildings are simplified so that their very "emptiness" may be filled by what only the Holy Presence itself can make meaningful. "This is none other than the house of God"—and God is Pure Spirit, and we who worship him "must worship in spirit and in truth."

An 'Image' Before Conversion—July 27, 1961

What drew me to the Church was her worship and her preaching. To be sure, I was living in New York and the best was at my doorstep. But I saw the same excellence at the Farm Street (Jesuit) church and the Brompton Oratory in London and its French version in Paris and Quebec.

Four churches in New York provided this early impression. The first was Our Lady of the Lourdes in Convent Avenue under Monsignor [Joseph] McMahon, where in addition to a superb liturgy a specialty was made of really great preaching. Here, for instance, every day in the Lent of 1930 I heard Bede Jarrett give his famous "House of Gold" sermons. These, too, were the days of Father [James] Gillis' prime and many a Sunday night would find me sitting under his pulpit in the great Paulist church. Here all one Lent I heard the famous Dr. [William] Orchard, the English convert. Then there was the Jesuit church a few blocks away from me in Park Avenue where at Vespers once could hear Ignatius Cox and Coleman Neville and men of their stamp. Corpus Christi, up near Columbia, was, I thought then and still think, one of the most exquisite churches I had ever seen. When I took my Anglican friend, the late Gregory Dix, to see it, he remarked, "Only sheer genius could have created all this beauty." The point is, the church itself and everything that went on there tugged insistently at the sleeve of the intelligent Anglican. Designedly, I wonder? Perhaps, and why indeed not? For Father [George] Ford knew well the Protestant, and especially the Anglican mind. To this day, I am told, the Sunday worship is the most intelligent and the preaching quite the best in New York. At any rate, all this was what I was used to in my own church—only it was better and because it was the Catholic Church, it rang true to me as my own did not.

The point I am trying to make is this: we cannot everywhere exhibit the urbanity and sophistication nor the degree of excellence found in these places. It is just as well that we can't, for the "image" they give is not typical. But we can and should insist on the principle which makes this picture of the Church possible. We can provide in the smallest and simplest of parishes a standard of music as fine as the Protestant's, because after all his best music, which he knows and sings better than we do, belongs to us. We can say and sing our Masses with care and grace. We can provide tasteful therefore beautiful, and not necessarily costly, vestments to please the eye— and do not say to me that this is not important. We can take our preaching more seriously than we do. We can put the best of our parish preachers in the pulpit at the principal Mass and if these are young men, we can let them preach often, even regularly, to give them the opportunity to develop their talent. I would not hesitate to advertise them by name and list their topics on a given Sunday in the weekend press as the Protestants do. This is what first attracted me to the Church and there are vast numbers of Protestants as interested and as hungry as I was in those days.

This Truly Glorious Church–September 2, 1966

Ten days or more ago I had the great joy of witnessing, in cassock and surplice and from the altar steps, the marriage of my godchild from the old days in St. Mark's Episcopal Church, New Canaan. Not the smallest measure of my joy was seeing for the first time under the happiest conditions this truly glorious church. I have studied Coventry Cathedral only from pictures, but of the two churches I will take this one.

The brochure which I was given by the rector describes it as "an attempt to express with modern materials"—bare brick being one of the best interior surfaces—"the fundamental Gothic design." Yet it is not a "Gothic style" church in any sense except in its height and massive strength. I should have urged, had I had anything to do with the building of St. Mark's, a shallower, perhaps fan-like, nave for liturgical and pastoral reasons; yet deep though the nave is, the difficulty is resolved by the superb elevation of the free-standing altar.

For the wedding the altar was handsomely arrayed in "Laudian" frontal (after the Anglican Archbishop Laud and the custom in the seventeenth century of covering the holy table on all four sides). The only lights were the majestic tapers at the four corners of the altar area. I think it unfortunate the fencing-in of this sanctuary by the communion rail, which to my mind tends to reduce the spaciousness that would otherwise be achieved.

The glory of the church, however, is the reredos and the glass. If memory serves me, my friend, Otis Charles, the rector of Washington, found this marvel of sculpture distracting. He thought it too "busy." I cannot agree with him. There is surely nothing like this screen in the world and I find it breathtaking. Here is, as the brochure describes it, "the drama of Redemption" and "the whole story of Christ's Church." Depicted in no fewer than 184 symbols applied on a screen of teakwood are God the Creator, God the Giver of the Law, God the Redeemer, God the Sanctifier, God the King and Judge, and Man's Response to God.

And then, the glass! To the north is the vast "Benedictine" window, in which the canticle "O all ye works of the Lord, bless ye the Lord" is treated abstractly in one sweeping composition—just in sheer beauty of glass and God's own sunlight singing as it were the hymn of creation. To the south in the chapel area are the windows of the Nativity, the Eucharist, and the Resurrection.

One extra-architectural feature of St. Mark's which delighted me was the working sacristy. I was shown through the cabinets for the vestments and the frontals by the head of the altar guild. The linens, all cared for by the women of the parish, were in immaculate order, as was everything used in the parish worship. Not the least of the treasures on display were the cushions at the altar rail, all done in the finest needlepoint by the women of St. Mark's. Then and there I determined to take some of my women down to New Canaan simply to open their eyes to the splendor of this kind of lay ministry.

It would be unfair, I think to conclude this report without mention of the plans for the Catholic church in New Canaan, St. Aloysius' "Alpha and Omega" church now in the building. You may recall seeing the architect's rendering in the Transcript a while back. I was taken past the site which to say the least is commanding. I have a feeling that before long there will be another reason, a good one, for a pilgrimage to New Canaan.

'New Churches of Europe'–February 25, 1965

This is a rare book and, I should think, for the architect and others charged with the building of churches, indispensable. What brought it to my attention was the notice, which you may have seen, that *Time* paid it a few weeks ago. I warn you: it is expensive, though not, considering what it offers and the high price of all books today, unreasonably so. Unless you, like me, find the new Christian architecture exciting, you won't want to own it; but do at least track it down—any first-rate library should be willing to buy it—and look at is more than 500 photographs. No book has given me greater interest and satisfaction in a long time.

It is a truism that the liturgical movement has had and is having a momentous influence on the architecture and the building of Christian churches. But if anything is calculated to demonstrate how really behind the times we in America are, and how contemporary and far-seeing are the builders in Europe, it is this book. To seek for the reasons for this I hesitate; yet I wonder how long it will take us to outgrow our chronic conservatism, our contentment with the derivative, our reluctance to catch up with the architectural vanguard of our times. In domestic architecture we have some examples to our credit; but in industrial buildings (witness cereal boxes in glass all over the "new" New York) and in Christian architecture we run a miserable seventh. Except for a very few churches (and most of these have been built by autonomous religious communities independent of episcopal censuring) we have little to our credit and it is unthinkable that our diocesan commissions, by and large, would approve the building in their dioceses of most of the churches shown in this book. To put it bluntly, a Le Corbusier would be unemployed in America. Prudence, that much invoked virtue, is so often only mistrust of innovation canonized.

From Austria, Denmark, England, Finland, France, Germany, Spain, Italy, the Netherlands, Norway, Sweden, and Switzerland some 60 churches are chosen and of these the greatest number are German. With few exceptions, notably a French church by Gillet and one or two of the Spanish churches, those in Germany seem to me to excel all the others. I was struck by how very poorly, as a truly contemporary church, the cathedral at Coventry comes off: apart from the great abstraction in glass, it has little to recommend it; it fails to be what a church should be today and this, I think, because of its deep-recessed choir and the resulting separation of the altar from the nave, surely a fatal error to perpetrate nowadays! In this matter, the compiler of the book is outspoken in insisting that the best place for the singers is the loft at the "west" end of the church.

What the reader and viewer of this book finds common to most of the churches shown is the marvelous "interplay" between the needs of public worship and the physical setting of the altar. More than forty years ago I heard what has always been for me the best definition of a church build-ing, (that is "a roof over the altar"—simply that, and nothing more). If you accept this simple criterion, you will not join the ranks of the many today who, looking at contemporary church say, "I don't like it. I want my church to look like a church!" Well, what does a church "look like," what should it look like? The building performs a function; it is not meant to be an image of anything—not a fish, not a ship, not a courthouse, not any one thing! Thus the designs of these churches follow no one principle. You find the cube and most of the other geometric solids. Floor plans are seen to be rhomboid, elliptical, square, oval. Interior arrangements of the seating, the placing of the entrances, the distribution of light—all these are arresting and all give evidence of careful thought to the accommodation of people within range of and generally round about the altar. Incidentally, how good it is to see a church furnished with chairs and not heavy, graceless pews! How much "lighter" is any nave as a result.

From New York my Episcopalian friend writes, "I suppose the 'great High Altar' is now a thing of the past, in its place, we seem now to have the great chopping block! Pity, I do not share this regret—it was he who last summer, seeing the cathedral in Toledo for the first time, burst into tears at the sight of the altar! Well, some are affected this way; I am not. And with the "great altar" gone, too, is pseudo Gothic, Puginesque, romantic, flim-flammery in "ecclesiastical" decoration. These churches are stripped absolutely of everything but what is essential to the offering of the divine mysteries. It will take a generation or two to do it, but this renewal of Chris-tian architecture, this rediscovery of what a church is meant to be, will go far to correct popular and peripheral devotions. What is basic to Christian nurture, what is fundamental to Christian faith—this is once more, slowly but surely, beginning to come into the light and into the consciousness of men's minds. What a wonderful day to be alive!

The Pangs of Adaptation–January 14, 1965

When it became clear some months ago that changes in the liturgy were certain, one of the questions I asked myself was how these would affect the music of the Church. It was for me a natural question because for much of my life I had heard English words sung to the traditional chants and hymn tunes of the Catholic Church. Despite the insistence of Catholic musicians that "it can't be done," I knew better; and after entering the Church I often wondered why our musicians did not take the trouble at least to listen to these most skillful adaptations against the day when they might be called upon to do a similar work. And I wondered, too, how the new order would affect monastic choirs whose chief daily work of prayer, after conventional Mass, is the offering of the Divine Office. Would Regina Laudis, Mount Saviour, and other communities, where the office is so scrupulously and nobly sung, change to English? This latter question was answered in part by a newsletter from Mount Saviour.

If you have ever been to Mount Saviour you know that here, since its foundation some 15 years ago, the current renewal has been anticipated in a score of ways. No surprise is this to anyone who knows its founder, Father Damasus Winzen, for he was reared in the school of Maria Laach and Pius Parsch. Not surprising either is the news that Mount Saviour has chosen to exchange the old ways for the new, since, as Reverend Father writes, "our standards are different from those of the average parish. On the other hand *we cannot ignore being part of the Church in this country.*"

This is surely good news, for here is one more of many services these scholars and specialists in worship and common prayer can do for priests and laymen alike. The sacrifices are great, for they are giving up a rare culture; the difficulties, they acknowledge, are enormous; but they have the courage and imagination to undertake them for the sake of the whole Church. Step one, it appears, is the recall of one of their priests from a new and daughter foundation. His experiments over the years with adapting and simplifying the chants will now be used to work the change. If so much is tentative and provisional at present, and if we must put up with a good and the bad—and much that comes my way seems to me to be bad—we can be sure that in the end something of fresh and permanent good will result. In the meantime, we do what we can.

Thanks to my skilled choir-mistress, the transition has been made (or, rather, is being made) with a minimum of difficulty. Using what I have learned from my Anglican days, we spent some hours one day adapting the simplest of the Mass melodies in our repertory to the official text—a text which, I cannot deny, is occasionally infelicitous and often un-rhythmical. The results were, we thought, amazing. No musician I, it seems neverthe-less to me that the genius of plain chant lies in its easy accommodation to the stress of the words, and not the other way round. The stress in the melody is put where it naturally belongs in the words when spoken. Thus, as an example of how not to adopt the chant, there came to us the other day from the Gregorian Institute a version of the Creed which, when I heard it, seemed to me extremely maladroit. And we discovered the reason: The adaptor had fitted the words to the traditional stresses. Thus, we sang, "THE Fa-THER" (PA-trem-OM) instead of, simply "the FA-ther." Once the stress was altered, the phrase became as natural when sung as when spoken. We made these changes of stress throughout the text and came up with a result altogether beautiful and flowing. This is what I mean by urging that our musicians listen to the work that has already been done and in use for now more than a century.

At the risk of being thought presumptuous, I will gladly risk comparison. Gladly will I match with anything now in use what my boys and girls and seniors do with the High Mass in English. It is as good, I dare say, as anything I have heard thus far or heard about. Moreover, the melodies are not the hasty improvisations of innovators but the ancient and matchless melodies of the chant. They are the same melodies my people in New York were able in a remarkably short time to pick up, learn, and finally to sing. Sunday by Sunday it was my joy to hear them "sing along" with the choir the entire Ordinary of the Mass—in English and to the Church's songs. I hope to have this joy again.

5

The Bible for Everyone

THE REALITY OF CHRIST in the bible is a mystery, a paradox, and a scandal. The death by crucifixion is subsumed into resurrection, a mystery for disciples then and believers now. The risen, spiritual, and incorruptible body was explained by the visionary St. Paul, and honest openness and sacrificial living by Christians of all eras will gradually make this clear. They do this in partnership with the Holy Spirit by whose action even human suffering, and thereby the incomprehensible, the fractured, and the tragic are transformed into life. Gordon takes on these high themes in his presentation of individual books.

In the Old Testament, nothing moved him more than the book of Job, where the spiritually unfathomable, the seeming victory of evil, and the suffering of the innocent are authentically questioned, but without loss of faith. Job's homage to God's allness was a prayer, and this ultimately made personal tragedies endurable. And in the New, Luke's gospel had a special place in his heart, for its tenderness and humanity: the infancy gospels, the raising of the widow's son, and the parables of the prodigal son and the good Samaritan. Gordon suggests that by reading Luke's Gospel and his Acts of the Apostles together—from the birth of Christ to the arrival of Christianity in Rome—readers can experience the great power of the good news. And only in Luke can be found the great canticles of Zachary, Mary, and Simeon. The psalms also were canticles he had enjoyed and been challenged by from his youth, through his seminary days (impressed by their sublime poetry) and in his Episcopal ministry (impressed by their effect on his parishioners). His great experience here were the classes taught by his old seminary dean, who revealed the depth of the ancient Hebrew mind as expressed in this poetry. As for the speaking in tongues reported in the Acts of the Apostles, he cites a modern Episcopal monastic bulletin article on the contrast between the initial childlike, open-souled self-expression of early Christians and the complexity and materialism of moderns. Now most often "tongues" is nothing more than a psychological strategy if not a quirk.

Gordon had strong opinions, indeed, about the parables: Christ didn't complicate them, and so explanations of them blur their original clarity, and here he spares not even the gospel writers for extended explanations and allegorizing—assuming that this was due to revisions made later to explain why so many in that first century had rejected Christ's teaching. Nor does he spare St. Augustine for transforming the good Samaritan parable into an elaborate spiritual world history. He decries biblical proof-texting: falsely conclusive arguments about central teachings from both the fundamentalist Protestant and pre-Vatican II Catholic side. The former, with their study group reading of texts with no life context led to a suffocating literalism, and the latter used biblical texts only to serve as proofs in theology manuals for Catholic seminaries. Rehabilitation of the original biblical text depends upon historical and literary analysis, which, he said, scholarly Anglicans and Protestants (Tillich, Niebuhr, and Barth) had already made clear.

For all the importance of bible study, only in the liturgy are the biblical readings lived and celebrated. They must be celebrated because Christ taught that eternal life begins now. The "liturgical year" presents and produces the reality of this life, following the story of Christ and entering into its mystery. The year begins four weeks before Christmas to celebrate the arrival, the Advent, of Christ in the world, and continues on through the events of Holy Week and Easter. For Gordon it was a year of grace, highlighted in his columns on seasons and Sundays. Advent was the beginning and the end of the year, marked by the presence of John the Baptist. Christmas bore Passiontide within it, because the Christ child is the same as the crucified Lord; indeed, Christ is the same in all the events of his life, and suffers today in the world's tragedies. He evokes the image of Christ's burial in the Washington, DC, National Cathedral because it portrays the majesty and beauty of a death that portends triumph. This triumph of the resurrection and ascension, on earth an amazing sight for the apostles and in heaven the coronation of Christ the king, is a triumph for humankind that has only to be claimed and lived.

Christ Crucified and Risen—March 26, 1964

During their lifetime the eleven (Judas having left their company) based their claim to be apostles on their having seen the risen Lord and, as their title plainly says, on their having been sent out to preach the good news of his victory over death. Thus when St. Paul, to the amazement of the infant Church, claimed apostleship, he justified his claim by invoking the same canon: he, too, on the road to Damascus, on his way to destroy the Christians there, saw Christ plain and was then and there commissioned to preach him crucified and risen. The risen Lord was St. Paul's watchword for the rest of his time on earth.

This explains why he, of all the writers of the New Testament, gives us the matchless words on death and the resurrection of the body. Take time out this Holy Saturday, the perfect "Sabbath rest" of the Christian, to read the 15th chapter of his first letter to the Corinthians: here, surely, is the best material for meditation in preparation for Easter Day.

"But some will ask," he writes, "how are the dead raised up and with what body do they come?" And he tells us. We cannot say that we know nothing of the resurrection body. We know far more that we at first suppose, and this even though the mystery is unfathomable in our life here below. St. Paul gives us four adjectives and these provide a key to our understanding. The new body in Christ, he tells us, is risen, spiritually, incorruptible, and glorious.

It is a risen body. But straightaway we meet a strange fact: namely, that not by all who say Christ risen, nor at once by any means, was he recognized. It was not until he spoke to her that Mary Magdalene knew him, you recall. And you remember that evening walk to Emmaus: how is it that the two disciples could have walked with their Lord, have listened to and talked with him at length, and yet have taken him for a stranger until he broke bread with them that night and they knew him? This is surely a mystery. We can only surmise that Christ hid himself even from his intimates so that by proofs more trustworthy by far more than human sight he might convince them of his risen self.

The risen body is spiritual. Whatever else this means, it means that it is no longer subject to the laws of physics and chemistry, no longer bound by time and space. It enters rooms whose doors are locked and bolted. It appears now here, now there, as though to get, as we say, from place to place were no longer a physical necessity. It simply is where it wills to be.

The risen body is incorruptible: what was "sown in corruption," that is, in the weakness and perishability of human flesh, what could suffer pain and bleed and finally die, is now beyond the ordinary frailty and extraordinary ravages of our mortal frame. Nothing can injure it; nothing limits it any longer.

Finally, this new body is glorious as once on the holy Mount it was "transfigured" by the radiance that hidden divinity gave it, so now the fullness of divinity overtakes it, masters it, and shines through it with dazzling, not to say, blinding, brilliance. Yet, though glorified—and this we must never forget—it still bears the marks of its passage through this world, the marks of the "passing over" from pain to death, to the grave, and on to the resurrection! "Behold my hands and my feet and my side," said Christ to doubting Thomas. The wounds of life's struggle to the death are not hid nor altogether erased, but made glorious and, so it would seem, unutterably beautiful. They are the pledge and earnest of our victory through Christ.

A body like unto Christ's risen body will be ours. By our Baptism, by our being members already of his Mystical Body, we here and now share in some of its powers and not a little of its beauty. This is the meaning and the promise of Easter.

'To the Holy Spirit and Us'—June 10, 1966

"It seemed good to the Holy Spirit and to us:" thus, in Acts, St. Paul makes decisions. Here in these words we have expressed the partnership between a Christian and the indwelling Spirit.

Every now and then one is amazed by the wisdom of his juniors in the faith. We lunched some time ago with a young man on his "alert" leave. He gave eloquent witness to what the Christian faith and life have meant to him through his boyhood and college years and to what they mean to him now as he confronts the unknown, quite possibly unpleasant, future. "The faith makes the *infinite* future so certain that the *immediate* future holds for me no fears." This, we take it, is what it means to live "in the Spirit;" for this young man the daily round and the common task all work together for good. "It seems good to the Holy Spirit and to him."

We could not help offering a word of caution, for youth cannot know all that life may hold out. We were thinking of countless distresses he cannot yet anticipate: those dread moments when a great test of courage comes, or great pain, or sorrow—moments when we know we are "in for it," and the agony is almost more than we can bear. Or the revelation, soon or late, that someone we had faith in and trusted we can trust no longer. Or the hurt given by one whom we love. Or the loneliness that is inseparable from some heroic choice we must make for God and for the right. It is at these times that we especially remember the Spirit's indwelling, his partnership with us throughout life.

"It seems good to the Holy Spirit and to us:" for the Spirit can and does hallow these moments of crisis, of decision, of pain. Then, also, we know that there are some things we cannot do or undo, some things we cannot change, lives we cannot control, destinies we cannot make or unmake. We must see all this in the conviction that God is nevertheless present in and through his Spirit whom we call Life-giver, Helper, Strengthener. With patience and this conviction we learn that things have a way of coming, as we say, "full circle." In the end *right will be done!*

If the Holy Spirit hallows the present and gives confidence for the future, he also redeems the past. How often do we look back and say, "This need never have happened. Or this ought never to have been. See what pain could have been avoided?" De we really believe that God can remake a human life or mend a broken relationship? It is, of course, the "Humpty Dumpty dilemma:" all the king's horses and all the king's men cannot put the poor, fragile, shattered egg together again. When in one's life that point is reached there is but one recourse. What seems "good to the Holy Spirit and to me?" Then it is, possibly after much suffering, that one learns that God allows some conditions to go on, and some mistakes to be made, and some failures to occur only because in this way, his children, learn. Then it is, if we will let him, that the Holy Spirit rushes in to cleanse and clarify, enlighten and fortify, modify, change, and correct our life. For he can set it going again stronger, wise, richer, more open to his love, better able to love and serve him in return. "It seems good to the Holy Spirit and to us."

The Absolute Rule of God—October 12, 1961

The lessons in the breviary from the *Book of Job* last month sent me back once more to reread the whole magnificent story. Nobody, it seems to me, not even two such poets as Archibald MacLeish and Robert Frost, can improve upon *Job* and I marvel that anyone tries. There are mysteries in the story—the providence of God, willed and permissive; the existence of evil alongside the good; the trials and sufferings of the innocent—and these no man can fathom. There is no need to bring Job up to date, for whether of our own time or of his own day, he is changeless. Bewildered he may be; agonize in body and spirit he surely does; but he holds on to a saving truth and it is this that makes him the man of God for any time and for any place.

He makes his own the primary truth that God rules. He believes steadfastly, with heroic and costing patience, that like the husbandman in the parable of the laborers in the vineyard, God can do what he wills with his own. "The Lord gave and the Lord hath taken away. Blessed be the name of the Lord." God, whose thoughts are not our thoughts, is inscrutable and his ways are past finding out.

There is no shortcut to positive thinking and confident living despite the persuasive powers over many of a popular writer on these matters. These blessings are not easily come by. They are not the assured result of "psychology" however soundly "applied." They come only to men and women of hard-wrought and persevering prayer and only after long and perhaps painful schooling in the first principle of prayer.

And what is this first principle? It is the conviction deep-rooted in the soul that one belongs more to God than to oneself; that one has nothing that he has not first received; that over what he is and has, he has only steward-ship and not ownership. Thus, my life is totally dependent upon God—dependent for this breath I am drawing and the next. Whatever befalls me of pain or trial, of gain or loss—these I know are for my good and come from a God whose name and will are love. My first thought this day will embrace this truth to the extent of my poor powers of mind and heart and will. My first homage today will be to him who is my light and life and salvation, in whom I, my surroundings, my work, my joys and sorrows, my associates and all others bound to me by affection or duty alone have meaning.

Essential, so the masters of prayer insist, if we would pray aright, is this first prayer every day. It needs no form of words, no special posture, though solitude and quiet are the ideal conditions of its making. It properly precedes, because it underlies, all other prayers, even thanksgiving and pe-tition. It need not take long, but it must be made.

The great Ignatius Loyola, near the end of his life, in a conference on prayer, said that were he to learn that his Society of Jesus was to be disbanded; that the work to which he had given life "*ad maiorem Dei gloriam*" was to be destroyed and come to nothing: he would ask only the boon of fifteen min-utes of prayer to settle his mind and to accept with joy the loving will of God.

This is prayer. But let no one pretend that it is easy.

On Reading the Psalter—December 17, 1965

Now that many of us are encouraging our people to read the "entrance song," the gradual and alleluia, or, as in Lent, the tract, the offertory and the communion verses of the Mass, something of profit may here be said about reading the Psalms, for these "intervenient," reflective readings are almost invariably taken from the Hebrew psalter.

The Psalms were our Lord's daily vocal prayer, as indeed they are of his Church. We have in the gospels only a few of what his life here on earth must have been uncounted allusions to them and quotations from them. How their imagery must have filled his mind and their language his speech! When we use them in our spoken prayers, it is no exaggeration to say that we are addressing the Father in the very words he used. (What better reason, then, than this for our using them?) Moreover, when we gather for worship and recite them in common, we are collectively the "voice" of his Body, the Church, continuing the praise he offered, the sorrow he expressed, the reparation he made in our name. He is our Head and we are his mouthpiece.

But using the Psalms as prayer, or even simply taking them up and reading them as the Word of God, is not always easy, especially at first. The other day a priest I know complained in my hearing that he "gets little or nothing" from reading the Psalms in English. (One wonders what he made of them in Latin!) And as he spoke I thought of my great good fortune in having first met the Psalms in an English version almost as early as I was able to read. I thought, too, of Dean Fosbroke's lectures on the Psalms in my old seminary. Steeped in Hebrew lore, no man I know has written or said anything to equal these discourses. For the Psalms are poetry and the Dean was a great reader and lover of poetry. Only if they are read as poetry can they be wholly appreciated or understood. And because they are the religious (and some of them, the national) poems of the ancient Hebrews, they are profoundly Jewish—in imagery, in outlook, in sentiment. If possible, then, the reader must enter into the Hebrew mind and think for the time being of himself, the world, and God as the Hebrew poet saw them. That this is possible I know, because with all the help I have had over the years, I have been able to do it. Having somewhat learned to do this, the reader must read these poems as our Lord must have read them; namely, as poems pointing to Christ, as poems about Christ and his people. Finally, he must learn to read and pray them as being in the "voice" of the Church at prayer—in praise and adoration of the Father, in penance and sorrow for sin, in home of future glory, in final and triumphant victory.

In my old parish in New York there was a woman who knew the psalter by heart. Of great age, she reminded me of Anna, the prophetess, who figures so charmingly in the gospel story of the Presentation. And like Anna, this woman "departed not from the temple day nor night." She was the first to arrive in the morning and the last to leave at night, winter and summer. As the day's psalms were read at Morning Prayer, before the parish Eucharist, and at Evening Prayer, at sundown, she would recite them with unfailing accuracy and without the help of a book. Once, when my curate was officiating at Evening Prayer, he lost his place by turning over two pages. Undaunted, Margaret (for that was her name) came in with the right verse and continued on until the young man found himself. We were all amused, you may believe. Another time she arrived late. We were reciting the day's psalter. As soon as she got within hearing distance, on her way up the aisle, she chimed in with the people's line without a second's hesitation. Well, this is one way, and a good one, to know the Psalms; but is the work of a lifetime.

Thank God for St. Luke!—October 14, 1966

Next Tuesday brings us one of the brightest feasts of October, that of St. Luke whom tradition calls "the beloved physician." How many readers of this essay will follow a suggestion; namely to read the gospel of Luke all the way through, if possible, at one sitting? Then, because his gospel is only the first of two books—the Gospel and the Acts—which carry the story from the birth of John Baptist and of the Christ, through his ministry, through the coming of the Spirit to continue his work on earth, down to the time when the Church had spread from Jerusalem to the center or empire, Rome, these should be read together as one continuous story. If you will do this, we guarantee a unique experience, an impression such as perhaps you have never had of the electrifying power of the good news, then as well as now.

St. Mark's symbol is the lion because his gospel—the first to be written of course—came upon the wilderness of the pagan world like the tumultuous roar of the king of beasts; Matthew's is the man because he traced the human lineage of the Son of God and was preoccupied with the sacred humanity; John's, the eagle, because his gospel, treating of the sublime doctrine of the Word made flesh, soars high above the realm of time. These signs are easy to read; but why should the author of the third gospel have as his symbol the lowly ox? It is a strange choice indeed.

St. Luke's is the most tenderly human of all the gospels and I am frank to own that it is my favorite. I never tire of reading it. Luke must have known our Lady well, or at least one close to her, for to him alone we owe the priceless stories of our Lord's childhood: the Annunciation and the Visitation, with her song *Magnificat* and Zachary's *Benedictus*; the Presentation, again with its canticle, Simeon's *Nunc Dimittis*; and the Finding in the Temple of the holy Child. But for Luke we should be the poorer for not knowing the raising of the widow's son, Martha and Mary, the woman who was a sinner, the company of ministering women, the rebuke of John, the ten lepers, Zacchaeus, the weeping over the holy city, our Lord's prayer for his executioners, the penitent thief, the journey to Emmaus, the Ascension. Then, the distinctly Lucan parables: the prodigal son, the good samaritan, the rich man and Lazarus, the pharisee and the publican, and the story of the importunate widow. It is Luke who enriched—artist that he is said to have been—our records of the Master by so many touches recalling his constant dependence on the Holy Spirit in his public work and his inner life; his constant practice of prayer; his horror of riches and love of poverty and the poor; the honor he paid to womanhood in the most deeply fallen and diseased as well as in the purest and the best.

All these stories and the deeds accompanying them are, as we say, "down to earth." They all have to do with the lowly of this world, even as Christ dramatized them by his own lowly condescension in coming quite close to our earth. The ox is immemorially the sign of lowliness, of the bearing of the burdens, of the nearness to the ground. The ox, too, was the animal of sacrifice in the Old Law. Is there not here much to account for the Church's choosing the ox as Luke's symbol?

For these—the evangelist and his sign and his subject—have a bearing on one another. Humility comes from *humus* and means "of the earthy." Our Lord gave the supreme example of humility. He bore man's heaviest burdens and made of them his sweet yoke. ("Take my yoke upon you," he said.) He is the Humble One. Whether St. Luke was the artist tradition says he was, or no, he has painted as has none other the human, the humble, the lowly, the pitying Christ in words that are as living today as when first he wrote them down.

On "Speaking in Tongues"—March 28, 1963

The phenomenon mentioned in the Bible, notably in the Acts of the Apostles, and elsewhere in early Christian documents, "speaking in tongues" is much in the news today It appears to have a vogue among other places on the campus at Yale. It is that altogether strange multi-lingual, often unintelligible expression of direct communication with God. With my editor's approval, I should like to publish here what is, I think, the soundest statement on the subject I have come across. It may be useful to some of us in the event we are asked about it. It comes from *Benedicite*, the latest issued of the little quarterly put out by Saint Gregory's (Anglican) Priory, Three Rivers, Michigan.

"The crux of the matter is that we are different people now from what we were in Biblical times, and some of the simple and direct means of opening communication with inner values and revelations are lost to us. We are told that Adam and Eve walked and talked with God openly and freely before the Fall; we have wandered still farther away from the simple and childlike openness of Biblical days and cannot depend on so direct and easy a revelation from God as was possible then. There still remain people on earth today who maintain the necessary childlike quality for revelation by 'speaking in tongues.' But for most of us that right has been lost.

"In a very simple person whose instincts remain near perfection, it is only necessary to withdraw the Ego-consciousness to induce a flow of revelation which is of great value to the personality. The irrational inner world flows out in nearly pure for to the great nourishment of the speaker. Such as person is inwardly 'clean,' without guile. To 'speak I tongues' is a valid and right experience for such a person; this was the condition where it possibility was encouraged in Scripture.

"But most modern persons have quite a different structure inwardly. The complexity of our lives, the materialism of our culture, the host of repressions which we all carry, all of these things have cost us the simplicity and 'cleanness' of our inner structure. When a modern person sets aside his Ego-consciousness, he is much more likely to let loose a flood of repressions and power drives which are anything but godly revelations. Even if he does contact a pure stream of revelation in himself, there will almost certainly be areas of darkness in his structure which can arrogate the new energy to their own uses. And, probably worst of all, if there is the slightest tendency to psychosis in the personality, it will be quickly aggravated without any mediating agent.

"The objection to 'speaking in tongues' is not that it is invalid; it is simply that we no longer have the necessary simplicity which can stand so direct and untampered a contact with great forces within us. We may think we are finding a direct and easy way to God on to find ourselves in the grip of evil!

"The great popularity of 'speaking in tongues' now is a sobering indication of the need for revelation and contact with inner realities. Man seems very prone to search for shortcuts, but there is no way to integration and revelation without the work, patience, and suffering which have always been associated with the Christian way. 'Speaking in tongues' is but the present form of shortcut which hypnosis, dianetics, 'truth serums,' and a host of other quick ways are representative. It is less dramatic to speak of prayer, worship, discipline, patience, intelligence, and faith, but these are the means which will take one closer to God than any of the quick and easy solutions."

This seems to me an admirable statement with which, I should suppose, the Christian psychiatrist would completely agree. One needs to break through the barricade of psychiatric jargon. For example, in the second paragraph of the passage, for "withdraw the Ego-Consciousness," I would read "forget self long enough." For "set aside his Ego-consciousness" in the next paragraph I would read "fail to act with right reason." For "integration" in the last paragraph, I read "wholeness" or "soundness" of mind, body and spirit. But one may as well ask the psychiatrist to dispense with the jargon of his profession as to expect the trained theologian to dispense with his specialized language.

Parables Masterstrokes—November 8, 1968

The Gospels of Matthew, Mark, and Luke abound in metaphors and similes drawn from nature or from everyday life which strike the ear of the mind forcibly and challenge it to active thought. These pithy sayings are invariably concrete rather than abstract. They are vividly pictorial, never vaguely general. Thus, we might say, generally and abstractly, "Charity should never be ostentatious." But how does Jesus say this? He says, "When you give your money away, do not blow your own horn on the street corner." Or, we might say, "Riches are a great hindrance to the practice of religion." How does Jesus put it? He says, "It is easier for a camel to go through the eye of a needle than for a rich man to enter the kingdom of heaven." The so-called Sermon on the Mount (Matt: 5 to 7:12) is largely a collection of sayings of this kind. These in turn are parables, so to speak, in embryo. And of this literary device our Lord was a master craftsman.

Now, this simple device is capable of development and application. For example, "A city set on a hill cannot be hid." And so, by extension, "men do not light a candle and put it under a bushel basket. No, they put it on a candle stand, and it gives light to the whole house. Let your light so shine before men that they may see your good works and glorify your Father in heaven." Be on the alert for this one in a few weeks from now: "When the fig tree puts forth leaves, you know that summer is near. So also, when you see these things begin to come to pass, you know that the kingdom of God is at hand." Nothing is more characteristic of our Lord's method of teaching than are these.

I remember a pupil of mine in a preaching class whose sermons far outshone those of all his classmates. I asked him where he had learned to preach as he did, for he was a delight to listen to and I found myself carrying his sermons in my mind for days after hearing them. His answer was, "I study our Lord's method. I try always to be concrete and pictorial; I avoid generalities and abstractions. I try to make my sentences as brief and telling as possible." There was really nothing I could teach him, but from him I learned a lot. This same trenchant public address is found in the preaching of the late Martin Luther King. If you come across the current paperback commemorative volume of his sermons, *Strength to Love*, buy it and read them.

There is, finally, the parable proper, the story built on a simple introductory saying. "The kingdom of heaven is like yeast which a woman took and hid in three measures of meal, until the whole mass of dough was leavened." Then come the somewhat longer stories like the Lost Sheep, the Hidden Treasure . . . What one regrets is the almost certain loss of multitudes of the sayings and stories of Jesus which simply did not survive long enough to be written down. But what does not the survival of the few we have tell of the skill of their creator!

Gospel Study: First Step—November 15, 1968

In St. Mark 4: 3–10 our Lord tells the parable of the Sower. Look it up and read it. Then the disciples ask, "What does this story mean?" And Jesus: "To you is given the mystery of the kingdom of God, but to those outside everything is told in parables, *so that they may look and look but never find, listen and listen but never understand, for fear that they should be converted and saved."* Does this sound like the Jesus who said, "Ask, and you shall receive; seek, and you shall find; knock, and it shall be opened to you?" We know it does not; and yet, in the more than 35 years I have been reading this passage in public worship, no one has ever confessed to me to being perplexed!

Here is one of the times when the evangelist, or perhaps a later editor, tampered with the original words of Jesus. Here is an instance of an attempt to "explain" or to allegorize a simple and straightforward story. And the attempt ends in nonsense. It is incredible that Jesus would tell a plain and simple story like that of the Sower and then say, "I tell this plain and simple story so that my hearers will not understand it. For if they understood it, they might profit by it and be converted." Incredible, I repeat, because entirely out of character. This was not our Lord's way, and whosoever they are, these cannot have been our Lord's words.

There follows the "explanation," the allegorical interpretation, ascribed by the writer to Jesus. But note: The seed is the word of God; yet "these" in the very next sentence become various classes of people—"These are they who". . . on the rocky ground . . . among thorns . . . and finally, on the good ground. I well recall the first time this was pointed out to me by my tutor at the seminary; like most, I had never really read the passage closely or critically, which is simply to say that I had never before really read it! And this was my tutor's way of introducing me to the science of the critical (*not* skeptical, *not* irreverent) study of the bible texts.

Well, then, what do scholars say about this? Because of certain "internal" evidences of certain words that have a very Pauline ring to them and that are not found elsewhere in the first three gospels, and considering the date of Mark, at least 30 or more years after the death of Christ, the experts ascribe this working-over of the parable to a writer of apostolic age. They think that the evangelist, or an editor, had to account for our Lord's failure to win his own people. Somehow it had to be shown, as early Christians believed, that the people to whom Christ came were blind and deaf to the meaning of his coming in order that God's purpose might be fulfilled by their rejection of him. Others go further and call this a frankly antisemitic bias on the writer's part.

Anyway, those who have followed me to the end have a first and easy lesson in gospel criticism. Perhaps some will be induced to explore a bit further.

How Not to Read Parables—November 1, 1968

Seeking much-needed relief those days from acrimony, controversy, and dissent, I have been turning to the New Testament, rereading some of my once familiar textbooks, going over class notes taken more than 35 years ago, and in general refreshing my memory on the critical data and methods associated with what we called in those days "the synoptic problem." This last is simply the attempt by scholars and experts to answer the questions, "How did the first three gospels come to be written, when, and by whom?"

In C.H. Dodd's The Parables of the Gospel I came recently upon something I had forgotten, that is, the fondness the Church Fathers had for turning the parables of Jesus into elaborate allegories. (How *not* to read the parables!) This prize example is from St. Augustine on the story of the Good Samaritan. And to think that this sort of thing was once—and until not so long ago—taken seriously! It makes incredible, highly amusing, reading. "A certain man went down from Jerusalem to Jericho:" the man is Adam and the city is the heavenly Jerusalem, the city of peace from whose blessedness Adam fell. "Jericho" means the moon, sign of our mortality since the moon rises, waxes, wanes, and then dies. The "thieves" among whom the man fell on his journey are the devil and his angels. These "stripped" him of his immortality; they beat him by persuading him to sin. They left him "half-dead;" that is, man lives in so far as he knows God, but because he is wasted by sin, he is only half alive.

The "priest" and the "levite" who passed by on the other side are the ministry of the Old Testament, profitless for salvation. Samaritan means "guardian," and this signifies our Lord himself. Binding up the man's wounds is the restraint of sin. The "oil" poured on the wounds is the balm of hope; the "wine," the impulse to good works.

The "beast" on which the victim is carried is the flesh in which God consented to come to us. The "inn" is the Church, the place of refreshment for pilgrims on the way to heaven. The "morrow" marking the return of the Samaritan is time after the resurrection of the Lord. The two "coins" are the promise of this life and of the life to come. The "innkeeper" is the Apostle Paul. The promise of additional payment, a work of supererogation, is Paul's council to celibacy.

Now read St. Luke, chapter 10, verses 30 and following. The young lawyer, "willing to justify himself," asks the question, "And who is my neighbor?" Jesus tells a simple and straightforward story, one that has all that is necessary, and nothing that is unnecessary, to make its point. A child can easily commit it to memory; nor is the point lost on the child, as I so well remember. Yet the story is inexhaustible; one goes back to it again and again throughout one's life to convict oneself of want of charity and to put oneself time and again under the judgement of the gospel.

I would not here suggest that there is no place for Christian allegory. Christianity and the world of literature would be the poorer without, say, Bunyan's *Pilgrim's Progress*. But the parables need no fussing over; they stand alone. Yet, as we shall see, even the evangelists could not resist the temptation to "explain" them—and in doing so did them a disservice.

The Current Revolution—January 27, 1967

It was bound to come. I mean, the unavoidable conflict between the traditional and 400-year-old views on matters theological and scriptural and the results of the scientific criticism of the Bible. The problem, of course, is to contain the revolution and make it productive of good, and not to let it issue in revolt.

Perhaps from the lofty height of my years and from my experience over the years I can write and encouraging word or two to some of my young friends in the priesthood whom I know or feel to be confused and challenged by the "new" (it is really not so new) learning. They are confused I believe, because they are quite unprepared to meet it, to assimilate it, and to make proper us of it.

A young priest comes to me with the news: "Father So-and-so has come to the point of rejecting most of the New Testament miracles;" or, "So-and-so is reading the Protestant theologians and is not sure now what he believes or whether he believes anything;" or, "What do we do now that the historicity of the Fourth Gospel is in serious doubt?" I try not to be complacent as these questions are put to me, although I have heard them all before; I keep calm and point out that I have lived with these ideas and problems for upwards of 35 years and am not in the least disturbed by them. I point out that our scholars are now just catching up with discoveries that have been taken for granted by their Protestant colleagues since the turn of the century.

I remember vividly my experience at St. Mary's Seminary in our first-year Scripture course. The tract on inspiration, as it was presented to us, seemed to me to be quite untenable, perilously outdated, and due in time to work a lot of mischief in the minds of the young men who, without a single question, without a suggestion of critical enquiry, swallowed the presentation whole. I recall our young professor's telling me (he had a doctorate in scriptural studies!) that I could not hold the "4-document" structure of the Pentateuch (and officially, in those days, we couldn't), which meant my having to delete from a paper I was writing any reference to it. And yet I knew with certainty that these critical discoveries were true, that became obvious to any student with even the most elementary critical apparatus. And so I kept my peace and my balance because I knew also that one day the truth would "out," and that the Church would one day have to come to terms with it. That day arrived—late, but not, thank God, too late.

As for the Protestant theologians: again I have to smile, for one would suppose that they had just come upon the scene. Tillich, Niebuhr, Barth and others were all in their prime while I was at General Seminary. Union Theological, their sanctuary, was only a short subway ride uptown. The two seminaries enjoyed each other's facilities and privileges. Indeed, I almost think that for my generation the intellectual preparation for the postconciliar era upon which we are entering was given at G.T.S. Our dean, an intellectual giant among giants in those days, read everything on both sides—the eminent Protestant theologians and critics, as well as the French and German Catholic scholars who in those days had to smuggle their papers and articles through the scholars' underground.

We were taught two things: one, never to be afraid of the truth, but with this caution, that we let time sift the permanently true from the possibly true; and second, never to doubt the continuing experience of the Spirit-dwelt Church, the only and ultimately certain "proof" of Jesus, the Christ, and his claims. It was this last which the men at Union did not have; our having it meant all the difference between darkness and light. And so, when young men come to me, as occasionally they do, this is what I try and tell them. And I tell them, while they are reading Tillich and Robinson and the others to read Newman, too. For Newman stuck it out, possessing his soul in saintly patience and calmest trust, the while he pursued holiness in life. (And I am by no means sure that this last is not the key to the whole problem!)

The Uses of Bible Study—November 22, 1968

As to the study of Church history, so to the study of the Bible: there has been added an ecumenical dimension. Let me try to explain.

From the little I have observed of the typical "Bible Study Class" in the American Protestant tradition, this undeniably reverent but not always legitimate use of the Scriptures, especially of the New Testament, encourages a fundamentalist reading of the texts and serves often to defend a purely sectarian position. Not long ago I watched an "evangelical reformed" layman take his New Testament out of his pocket—it was an interleaved edition whose alternate pages were minutely annotated in delicate script—and heard him skillfully trace the "evidence" through the Gospels, the Acts, and St. Paul, which to his satisfaction confirmed his faith in his own Christian denomination and demolished the centuries-old defense of the Catholic Church. I have observed the same procedure before a large congregation in New York's Calvary Baptist Church.

Yet it is not to be overlooked that we Catholics have made similar use of the Scriptures. If our laity has been spared, through non-exposure to the Bible, the "Bible and Bible only" view of the Christian faith, certain it is that our apologists have for centuries used the Bible for polemical and defensive purposes. I remember my amazement when, at the Catholic seminary I was sent to, I found the "tracts" in theology and apologetics crammed with "proof texts." A given position would be taken or a proposition be stated and then to support these one would find the "proof from Scripture." And by no means always could the text cited bear the burden of proof! This, surely, is a questionable method as is the one described earlier.

Thus on both sides the Scriptures have been manipulated to serve particular and oftentimes hostile points of view. It is now the time for all of us, all Christians and not least ourselves, to ask, "What *in fact* do the Scriptures say? What *in fact* do we find in the New Testament?"—about all manner of things. The scholars alone have the answers and we should do well to listen to them. From now on Bible study has a new, an ecumenical, dimension.

From this kind of Bible study we shall all profit in the end. We shall have to put aside for the moment our misreadings of our several histories, our inherited bias, our "tendenz," and address ourselves quite objectively and calmly, to questions like these: What in fact did our Lord say on such-and-such matter? What in fact happened at the Last Supper; what was his meal and what use did he make of it; how and with what meaning was it continued by the Christian community? Or: what kind of Church do we in fact find in the Acts and the epistles: what in fact was its organization; what were the nature and composition of its ministry; what kind of authority did it exercise; what did it take to be its mission? . . .

The answers to these and many other crucial inquiries we shall find highly provocative, often disturbing. But a scientific and critical rereading of the New Testament can do much to hasten the day of Christendom reunited.

Eternal Life Here and Now—April 20, 1961

Reread St. John's Gospel and you will see what makes his proclaiming of the good news different from all the others. St. John convinces you that the life of heaven, born of grace, begins not after death but here and now. He insists on this again in the opening words of his first epistle: "I write of what was from the beginning, what we have heard, what we have seen with our own eyes, what we have looked upon and our hands have handled, of the Word of Life. And the Life was made known and we have seen, and now testify and announce to you, the Life Eternal which was the Father, and has appeared to us."

It is the function of the Church to reproduce faithfully this very life of our Lord. It is the Church's function to present before the world and to her members not the earthly life only but the complete life—the earthly having its completion in the risen and the heavenly. Not only does the Church reproduce this life before our eyes; it conveys it to our minds and nurtures it in our souls.

Thus, the Church year, with its recurring seasons, its regular comings and goings, its variety of feasts and fasts, its cycles of rite and ceremony, is one of the means—it has been called the primary means—of both this reproduction and communication. Each year we reenact together the events of our Lord's sacred life. There is a wide sweep of activity, covering the entire twelve-month, and this is designed with nothing short of inspired genius to correspond faithfully to the thirty and three years of Christ's life. Yet at the same time this activity communicates to us the powers which Christ through his life, death, and resurrection gave to men.

There is in the cycle of the Church's worship year by year a marvelous blending, a kind of interpenetration, of the temporal and the eternal, of the earthly and the heavenly. Here in this sacred round of worship heaven and earth overlap. The boundary between the two worlds is indistinct. Life flows back and forth from one to the other without need of passport or visa. We are occupants of one realm and citizens of the other, colonials of the mother country, and yet at home in both.

Just as our Lord lived in the world as man and yet never for a moment forgot his essential divinity, so the Church, obliged to live in the world, is nonetheless always aware of the true meaning and source of her life, God. The Church, too, moves in both spheres, moves from one to the other without let or hindrance, almost unconsciously. Just as our Lord was both God and man, and altogether God and man, so his Church is both God and man. And while she continues to fulfill her span in this world, she will always, as did Christ, exhibit the life of the one by exercising the powers of the other.

We, then, have come in Eastertide to the climax of the Christ-life. We are in the midst of the great Fifty Days ("All your pagan feasts put together," said Tertullian to his world, "cannot begin to equal the splendor of the fifty days between Easter and the Ascension"). As in years past we have come more and more to know and understand the Christ-life through the Church's worship; so this year we have learned more and explored deeper into the realm of its great mysteries. This, in a word, is what we mean when we say that we have had a good Lent and a blessed Easter. Ours is truly the life of heaven.

Self-Emptying of God—December 27, 1968

I cannot remember where or when I first heard or read this, but it has stayed with me most of my life: "God never showed himself so great as when he made himself small." Christmas celebrates this "self-emptying" of God. Fully understood, then, Christmas should unlock for us the secret of the fullest life possible. How otherwise could this be since this was the kind of life the God-Man chose to live?

But what if the sophistication we have perhaps all unknowingly acquired in our adult years should obscure from our sight today the simplicity, the "smallness," of the Christ Child? We should not like to think that we are so worldly-wise as to be contemptuous of the truly wise. Or that we are so smart as to find the company of the simple dull! Or that we are so carefree as to find the hard life of Mary and Joseph a bore. Or that we are so comfort-bound and luxury-loving as to fail to pity the Child who chose a manger and the straw of the field for his cradle and the house of a poor man for his home.

Yet, though we would wish it otherwise, this may well be our plight. I know that it is mine.

Gerald Manley Hopkins once wrote of the mystery of the Incarnation: "Christ is in every sense God and in every sense man, and the interest is in the locked and inseparable combination; or rather, it is in the person in whom the combination has its place. Therefore, we speak of the events of Christ's life as the *mystery* of the Nativity, the *mystery* of the Crucifixion, and so on of a host; the mystery being always the same, that the Child in the manger is God, the culprit on the gallows God, and so on. Otherwise birth and death are not mysteries; nor is it any great mystery that a just man should be crucified. But that God should be fascinates—fascinates us with the interest of awe, of pity, of shame, of every harrowing feeling."

"Of every harrowing feeling." My own struggle, I find, is trying to reconcile the simple, homely joys of Christmas—children, the family hearthside, friends, the giving and receiving of presents, the table dressed and heavy with food—with the world's agony. The former are luxuries which the few enjoy—and I happen to be among them. The agony all over the world is the norm—and I know little or nothing about it.

I find, for example, almost insupportable the irony in the very word *Bethlehem*: "House of Bread." (*Bread,* of all things!) I recall that my God chose to be born in the "House of Bread," in the rudest poverty, of a despised people, knew exile and homelessness, had no place whereon to lay his head, died an ignominious death. And then, in my prayer, I put Bethlehem—House of Bread—alongside words like Vietnam, Harlem, Watts, India, Biafra.

And then I look about me, and at myself and my condition and my way of living. "Every harrowing feeling" indeed! How can I understand, how can I hope to share, the common agony of mankind? "Until the whole world is clean," wrote Hawthorne a century ago, "we are all unclean." This is my torment on Christmas Day.

I do not quite despair, because I try to remember that I am a Christian. Yet I wonder, too: how does one man like me, at my age, dare to hope to be simple again, to have true poverty of spirit, to regain some small semblance of his innocence, to mourn with those who mourn, to feel something of the pain of the world's crucifixion? How, I wonder, like my God, to be so great as to be willing to become small?

A Meditation on Death—April 9, 1964

In the chantry of Washington's Anglican cathedral, in a chapel under the dedication of St. Joseph of Arimathea, there is above the altar a painting of the burial of our Lord. The procession is making its way to that tomb "wherein never man has laid." It is by St. Joseph in whose hands is the Cup of the Upper Room and in whose bearing is that grave care he had for the body of the Lord. The abrupt descent has led from distance Calvary. Those bearing the body have reached a point directly in front of the observer. Hence, the body of the Lord, magnificent, serene, strong and beautiful in death, is the first thing one sees. Here, at the lower right, is the centurion; his head is bowed and he leans on the lance. Behind and above the bier stands the Mother of Sorrows. With her is John. Others whose identity one can only surmise complete the group of attending mourners. So it is back to the Lord in death that the eye returns. One now sees the wounded hands, the riven side. One remembers the violence of the death so lately inflicted, yet one cannot deny the majesty of death itself, so eloquently is it here set forth. A darkening sky over all is shot through with burnished gold. Both darkness and light are here. The colors are those of Christian death: black for sorrow, scarlet for martyrdom, green for hope, and gold for victory.

Here is all the majesty and beauty of death. Here is sorrow in strength and strength in sorrow. Here is that godly, uniquely Christian reverence for the dead and the sorrowing. Yet there is no suggestion here of finality, for the sky, though dark and threatening, promises a bright tomorrow. The setting, sinister and forbidding as at first it would appear, is peopled with men and women of prayer. In this painting we may overlook no single aspect of this deep mystery of death. Nor can we forget that this small gathering of men and women was the Church of Christ on Good Friday. Here was Christianity—on its way to a tomb.

There is this striking difference between the Church of Good Friday and the Church of Eastertide. We are the latter. It is as the Church risen and triumphant that we have for example, the gospel on one of the Sundays in Eastertide: "And Jesus said, a little while and ye shall not see me; and again, a little while and ye shall see me, because I go to the Father." We read this with the knowledge of what soon came after; we hear it knowing, as they who first heard it could not have known, what it meant. We hear it knowing how the fact of death, the closing of the yawning gates of the tomb, deprived them of one kind of sight; and how, later, in what took place, they were given another kind of sight—the true vision of insight, the power to look through, behind, and about the physical facts. "You shall weep and lament and be sorrowful, but your sorrow shall be turned into joy."

We, then, hear these words of our Lord as believers, as heirs of the Resurrection, as those who know that in Christian death there is no less sorrow because there is also an element of joy, but rather, greater joy because there is a true and abiding sorrow. As heirs of the Resurrection we understand how apt are the words, "A little while . . ." We hear these words today and for us, in a world so filled with and so conscious of violence and death, the sting of death is by more than a little removed. "If thou hadst been there," said Martha, "our brother had not died." "Thy brother shall rise again," said Jesus. "I know that he shall rise again, in the resurrection, at the last day," said Martha. "I am the resurrection and the life . . . believest thou this?"

What, therefore, do we take reality to be? What in this life is waste, and what is gain? What is it to live in the real and eternal sense? O death, where is thy sting? O grave, where is thy victory? To look on Christ in death—to be mindful of his resurrection: this is the answer to the most important question we can ever ask ourselves.

And a Cloud Received Him—May 24, 1962

It is a faithful and true saying, one to be believed if we would be saved through Christ, that he, forty days after his resurrection, in his risen and glorified body, went up into heaven and took his place at the Father's right hand. "And while they beheld, he was taken up, and a cloud received him out of their sight."

That is all that is said. Many speculate about it, but the fact is, what the apostles saw with their astonished eyes they put with admirable economy into words to express what must, to say the very least, have been an amazing sight.

Our Lord's ascension was straightaway coupled in the apostles' preaching with his resurrection. He was now not only risen but glorified; he was all that "Messiah" meant: "he who was to come," he who now is crowned with kingly glory. We may think of the Ascension as the feast of the Coronation of Christ as King.

So also does the Church recall this daily at Mass: "in memory of the blessed passion of the same Christ our Lord, of his resurrection from among the dead and of his ascension to heavenly glory." What the mind cannot take in, nor the tongue fully tell, our common worship makes present and fulfills.

We can, however, feebly, try to understand what our Saviour's return to heaven must have been. It was a homecoming, a victor's triumph, to rejoice the blessed spirits in heaven—the mighty angelic host, the patriarchs who had seen him go, the prophets who had foretold his sojourn on earth: all these now hailed him with greater joy because it was a new joy they took in him. They had never before seen him in the splendor of his manhood. The Son of Man, fashioner and father of his new creation, the Church, heir to the heavenly throne, now returns to share the sovereignty with his Father. It was this he had prayed for as his darkest night on earth drew near: "And now, O Father, I come to thee. Glorify they Son with the glory he had before ever the world was." He comes home bearing now a human body—a body once wracked and torn by the passion; a body bearing even now the five sacred scars; yet a risen body, transfigured, incorruptible, full of power, radiant.

Here, then, is the first point of our meditation as we prepare for the feast. Not alone that he is king, for in heaven his sovereignty is ever unquestioned. Not alone that he is lord of all the earth, for "the Lord is king, though the heathen rage and the peoples be impatient." Not this only, but that he makes us also "kings and priests." "I go," he said, "to prepare a place for you, that where I am, there you may be also." Leading captivity captive, he shares his royalty with us; he gives us power to become the sons of God; we are co-heirs with him of the kingdom. We are, in the words of Peter, "a royal priesthood, a peculiar people, a holy nation."

The Ascension is our victory as well as Christ's. Our human nature, now redeemed, is a kingly nature. It is not, therefore, to be despised, exploited, enslaved, nor [any whit] abused, for it is "bought with a price"— and at what cost!

6

Spiritual Life and Christian Mission

If the spiritual gold standard is the apostolic Christian, each one called to be another Christ, the opposite would be the guilty bystander, denounced most passionately when Gordon saw such guilt in himself and his fellow American Catholics. Citing Christ's sorrowing over all the destruction of Jerusalem for the guilt of some, Gordon lists prejudice against African Americans, ill will, scapegoating on the part of some as elements of American national guilt. His admonitions, biblically supported of course, reference first of all Thomas Merton, who popularized the label "guilty bystander," and then Paul Tillich, who said that only total repentance counts and only God can effect total forgiveness.

Ranging widely, Gordon presents Tolstoy's *War and Peace* in the character of the anti-war officer Prince Andrei to show that war is the greatest sin of all, and declares that now is the opportune time for bishops and pastors everywhere to condemn war. He is pleased that Pope Paul VI has started—if halfheartedly—the process; he is one with the pacifists he knew personally, such as A. J. Muste, and Dorothy Day and regrets his own failure to preach pacifism. But the strongest book recommendation he ever made was for James Baldwin's *The Fire Next Time,* a personal narrative-manifesto on the destructiveness of white and black violence.

For exploring the great dogmatic themes, Gordon drew upon the writing of clerics who had inspired him, such as George Tyrrell, the good Catholic priest condemned by Pope Pius X for "modernism," on the meaning of the cross. For Tyrrell, the just person is to a society what conscience is to the individual and serves to oppose surrounding evil. Only the perfectly just Savior, however, could process the world's evils through his heart, redeeming humankind in spite of itself. This, God's total acceptance of humankind, was excellently preached by Miles Yates, chaplain of General Theological Seminary one Easter, as Gordon remembers it. The tax collector Zacchaeus, the woman taken in adultery, and the penitent thief were accepted not because of their worth but in spite of their unworthiness. More "down-to-earth" but of unequaled importance for human beings is the marriage counseling of Robert Farrar Capon, a gifted and privileged Episcopal pastor and seminary director, whose own marriage and love of his children is the core motivation of his book.

Inasmuch as individual writers cannot and do not offer complete solutions to life's problems, the apostolates of contemplative and missionary communities can leaven whole societies. On the contemplative option, Gordon offers the experience of an old Anglican friend who could find the richness of Christian mission only in Trappist contemplative life—there being nothing comparable in Anglicanism that worked for him. And the "Ignatian" (Loyola!) option can provide light along the way, especially for those haunted by their own guilt. Here Gordon offers St. Ignatius's theology of memory with its emphasis on God's forgiveness as the solution.

Official Christian ministries—lay people and priests together—express this multiform spiritual vitality. In the church, the priestly ministry would be ineffective, would barely exist, without the lay people, whose competence is vital for the spiritual and material progress of the parishes, so they should be given an essential say in the running of the parish in accordance with their areas of expertise. What may be overdone in some Protestant communities, is underdone is Catholic parishes.

Gordon profiles the three great callings of priest, doctor, and teacher with examples and explanation—undoubtedly recalling his own father as he gives most attention, if not pride of place, to the doctors, so often Christlike, whatever their faith. He dedicated a column to the young paralyzed but active teacher and coach at his old prep school Phillips Andover; this teacher trained his students to value the underprivileged, and urged the administration and alumni to promote a more diverse student body. No individual or group in Christian education deserved more gratitude than Catholic teaching sisters, whom Gordon elaborately praises for dedication to teaching, their own studies, daily convent tasks, and especially for the personal good qualities passed on to students. He does not forget here the great contributions of nursing sisters and contemplatives.

But the priest surrounded by his parish should be the ground and source of spiritual life and Christian mission, and Gordon would have young priests—whose enthusiasm he often lauds—aware of those faithful parishioners such as his own elderly parishioner, a churchgoer since his youth, a parish founder as an adult, and worshiping there with his son on the day his wife passed away.

I'm the Guilty Bystander—June 14, 1968

I am Thomas Merton's "guilty bystander."

There is such a thing as a national, a corporate, a people's guilt. All through these late fearful and fateful hours the words of Christ's grieving over his city have coursed through my mind: "O Jerusalem, Jerusalem, you kill the prophets and stone those sent to you. Yet how often would I have gathered you together as a hen gathers her chickens under her wings, and you would not. Your house is left desolate because you would not know the things that belong to your peace."

Not every Jew who heard Christ's message wielded the hammer that drove the nails through the hands and feet of the Son of Man and on into the wood of the cross. But that the nation was guilty—"his blood be on us and on our children!"—there can be no question. And corporate guilt—a nation's, a people's, guilt—profound, deep-rooted, disguised, unrecognized, and therefore all the more terrible—is a sickness. I am a guilty bystander, afflicted with my country's guilt.

For so long as I allow prejudice and ill-will to lodge in my heart I am guilty: guilty of a terrible injustice which God will not long suffer.

For so long as I will not be my brother's brother, I am guilty: guilty with the bloodied guilt of Cain.

For so long as I lack the guts to lay it on the line, in the pulpit where I am sent to preach the gospel of Christ, I am guilty: guilty of the cowardice of a Judas.

For so long as I refuse to sit down and reflect on the awe-ful meaning of the recent tragic events, and of all that has led up to them, and of all that may well follow them; for so long as I will not read them in the blinding light of their Scriptural import; I am guilty: guilty of the deadliest kind of spiritual sloth and of moral decay.

For so long as I admit into my heart the fear of the black man, which in turn becomes my hatred of him, I am guilty: guilty and, therefore, the object here and now, where I sit secure and safe and at my ease, of the divine displeasure and the awful judgment of a righteous God.

For so long as I refuse to be prophetic and truth-telling and instead take recourse in a fatuous chauvinism, I am guilty: guilty of betraying myself, my priesthood, my people, and my God.

For so long as I look for the scapegoat—"the Communist conspiracy" is the readiest at hand—so that I may embalm my conscience in the sleep of death, I am guilty: guilty of self-deception and spiritual suicide.

There is a corporate guilt. My nation is gravely ill. And I—I am the guilty bystander.

Is It A Blessing Or A Curse?—August 25, 1967

In a collection of memorable sermons, *The Eternal Now*, Paul Tillich gives two definitions, one of repentance and the other of forgiveness. "Genuine repentance," he says, "is not the feeling of sorrow about wrong actions, but it is the act of the whole person in which he separates himself from elements of his being, discarding them into the past as something that no longer has any power over the present." Then, further on: "But the meaning of the (past) can be changed by the eternal, and the name of this change . . . is forgiveness."

Everybody's past has something in it both of blessing and of curse and of emptiness. Hence, the pathetic struggle over our past that goes on in most of us. The curse of the past can only be healed by repentance. The burden of the past becomes a blessing only when it is lifted and removed by the transforming blessings of forgiveness. So much for the personal experience which we have all known.

It is, however, when the preacher applies this principle to our nation that the sermon hits home. Our country, perhaps more than any other nation in all history, has received many and great blessings from its past. Yet from its earliest days there have been elements at work that have been and still are a curse. Its handling of the problems of race within its borders and in dealings with other peoples abroad is in our day the most conspicuous example of this. "'The American way of life,'" says Tillich, "is a blessing of our past, but it is also a curse which poisons the present and threatens the future."

"Can a nation," he asks, "have genuine repentance?" Can it separate itself from curses of past and present? Can a nation, can a people, undergo the transforming experience of forgiveness? The history of the ancient people of God and of the Church shows that this is possible even if rare, even if always painful. Will this happen to our nation? Can America or will America repent? Can we, or will we, know genuine repentance and that blessing of forgiveness? Pointed indeed is the definition of repentance if we substitute "nation" for "person,"—"genuine repentance is not the feeling of sorrow about wrong actions, but it is the act of the whole nation in which it separates itself from elements of its being, discarding them into the past as something that no longer has any power over the present."

An affluent American woman asked the other night in the hearing of an astonished audience, "Is anybody in America ever hungry?" Our astonishment was exceeded only by hers when she was reminded that the vast numbers of American families live on pet foods. A priest of my acquaintance contends with the naïveté of a child, "Nobody in America need be out of work." A woman, otherwise intelligent, asked me during the Detroit riots, "Why do these people behave this way?" Perhaps the most derelict Congress in all our history makes sport of the debate on rat control, makes itself appear more asinine than it already was. The nation's Administration plays brinkmanship in a war that is inconceivably mad and grows daily more senseless. The list is practically inexhaustible. Where is all this likely to end? Where will it lead our nation and ourselves? Is God well pleased with America? Shall we inherit a blessing or a curse? The Word of God— the prophets and the psalms especially—has the answer. He who reads may read it plain. But who bothers?

The Vilest Thing in Life—September 13, 1968

Readers of Tolstoy's panoramic novel, *War and Peace,* will recall the contrapuntal arrangements of its two themes: Domestic and social life among the Russian aristocracy in town and country; and war, in particular the Napoleonic invasion and brief occupation of Russia.

If, as is the view of many, this is the greatest novel in any language, not the least important aspect of this claim would be the author's reflections on war. Tolstoy saw war as the scourge of mankind, "the vilest thing in life." Taking one war, and an especially devastating one, with all that accompanies it—the sufferings of the peoples, the burning of towns, the slaughter of thousands upon thousands of men, the laying waste of the land, the stupidity of the leaders—Tolstoy applied his view of this to all war. That he believed wars to occur and recur not so much by the will of men as by a set of fatalistic, cyclical, and mysterious "laws," is not the point: Tolstoy was essentially a moralist and not a mystic.

Of the spectacular cast of characters, the person of young Prince Andrei is perhaps the most winning. In a conversation with his friend, Pierre, on the eve of the battle which inflicted a fatal wound, Andrei makes the following observation on war as he has come to know it: "There is no profession held in higher esteem than the military. And what is war? What makes for success in warfare? What are the morals of the military world? The aim and end of war is murder; the weapons employed in war are espionage, treachery, and the encouragement of treachery, the ruining of a country, the plundering and robbing of its inhabitants for the maintenance of the army, and trickery and lying which all appear under the heading of the art of war. The military world is characterized by the absence of freedom—in other words, a rigorous discipline—enforced inactivity, ignorance, cruelty, debauchery, and drunkenness. And yet this is the highest caste in society, respected by all. Heads of state wear the military uniform and bestow the greatest rewards on the man who kills the greatest number of his fellow creatures. Tens of thousands of men meet—as they will tomorrow—to massacre one another, to kill and maim, and then they will offer up thanksgiving services for having slain such vast numbers (they even exaggerate the number) and proclaim a victory, supposing that the more men they have slaughtered the more credit to them. Think of God looking down and listening to them? . . . life has become a burden to me of late. I have begun to see and understand too much. It doesn't do for a man to taste of the tree of the knowledge of good and evil."

This was 1812. But times and men's minds and war have not changed. Yet this is the scriptural view of war, "the vilest thing in life." Is it not opportune for an outright condemnation of war by Christian leaders—not just by one man, but by all? Our bishops to a man, all bishops and pastors everywhere?

Birmingham and Pentecost—May 30, 1963

How is it that Negro children of kindergarten age can walk calmly through jeering, cursing, and spitting mobs of whites to get to school? According to James Baldwin it is because they have behind them and all about them an intimate knowledge and an atmosphere of suffering. It is their tradition and their daily experience of life in America. It is the milieu into which they are born and their daily bread. It is their claim to greatness and nobility, as it is the hallmark of every man or woman grown to the measure of the stature of Christ, the Suffering Servant. It is their distinctive contribution to what little there is of a genuine, maturing, and mature culture in our society.

No admirer am I of James Baldwin as a writer of novels. In fact, of his latest I read some 50 pages before I carried the book out to my trash can. Yet Baldwin is brilliant and able. He is exceedingly aware, far more than I can claim to be, of the neuroses and psychoses of our age. But he wants restraint and discipline and a sense of proportion that is, if he would use the novel effectively to mirror the convulsions that have overtaken us.

However, *The Fire Next Time* is something else altogether. For it I give him A-triple plus. It is the most convincing and convicting, indeed the most terrifying, reading to come my way in a long day. It is absolutely real; there is not a phony sentence in it, it rings with the authenticity of a poet's and prophet's and a lover's insight. "A lover's, you say?" Yes, for it says much of love as the only and ultimate way to national harmony and domestic peace. Despite its rejection of Christianity, or rather what the author fancies Christianity to be, *The Fire Next Time* is a deeply Christian manifesto. And it is required reading—this I say even though I am the first to bridle when anyone says to me, "Here is a book you must read." Must I? In this instance: "Yes," say I, "you must."

This is no mere diatribe conceived in hatred and written in blood. Hatred, says the author, is too heavy a sack for the Negro to carry these days. He, like the white, must pay one day (and it is later than we think) the as yet unsettled account of racial warfare. Let no one pretend that it isn't warfare—declared and open war on both sides! Lest any be so foolish as to laugh off the fanatical movement, the "Nation of Islam," and Malcolm X, its second in command, he is advised to read Baldwin's sobering appraisal of their threat to our common peace—not, I hasten to add, to our "white" peace! Neither the movement nor its leaders can possibly succeed; but on the other hand, neither will hordes of Negroes hesitate to forsake Baptist allegiance once they are convinced of a racial mystique and a supernatural destiny. They will all too readily, and in frightening numbers, join up with the "holy war," the ethos of Islam, and embrace its age-old end, the extermination of Western whites.

This is a book, then, which everyone in public life—priest, minister, pastor, teacher social worker, industrialist, and politician—is bound to read if he would know the extent and the already white-hot heat of the fire smoldering beneath the tinder-dry surfaces of our American wasteland. The Senator Byrds of our time should know that essentially they are no different from the Malcom X's: both have one end in common—the setting of race against race, of black against white, with a view to the destruction of one by the other. This is no mere fanatical notion: it is a fearful and appalling fact.

It is not without design that God poured out his Spirit on Pentecost in tongues of fire. The fire proclaimed the burning love of the Sacred Heart, the love of the Suffering Servant, himself sprung from a race despised and rejected. Which, then, is it to be for Birmingham, for Chicago's South Side, for New York's Harlem with its "wine and urine-stained hallways and alleys," indeed, for all America? Is it to be a refining fire, a Pentecostal fire—or is it to be the destroying flames of a veritable hell on earth? Is it to be an America that knows neither bondman nor free, neither Greek nor barbarian, neither black nor white, but a people united and free, a people conscious of its dignity and of what could be its unique destiny, a people ready to become a holy priesthood after the heart and mind and will of Christ? This is the choice by which we stand or fall, the choice on which depends the blessing of God on us and on our children or the terrible visitation of his just vengeance.

'The Grand Idea of Peace'—December 22, 1967

Surely no civilized person in the "civilized parts of the world" (where, pray, are they?) will fail to warm to Pope Paul's "Day of Peace," the "idea" he has chosen to "launch" this Advent. If proof were needed, which it isn't, of his agonizing over the state of the world and of his concern for world peace, this would be enough.

Yet it was with difficulty that I read excerpts for his call to my people last Sunday: difficult because of the nearly intolerable "Vatican style," the tortuous, multi-complex sentences, the inflated and solemn-sounding idiom; but I wanted to prepare my people as far in advance as possible to make good use of this unique opportunity.

There was the (to me) most unfortunate paragraph—unfortunate because less than just, and in the context of the whole, irrelevant—on pacifism. I thought of the great A. J. Muste, of sainted memory, of Dorothy Day, of a host of pacifists I have known, whose life and witness are the contradiction of what the Pope has called "a base and slothful concept of life," as thought the true pacifists were an unproductive and irresponsible citizens. And by failing to do justice to the true pacifist, the Pope seems also to ignore the numberless men and women, young and old, including the entire Society of Friends, whose consciences force them to oppose war in any form, at any time, and most especially nowadays. It is these very persons who have "launched" this "grand idea of peace" for lo! these many years; and these, in a phrase I heard used the other day, have long been "putting their bodies where their mouths are." Can we, I wonder, in our time hope for a leader who will have the courage to condemn outright the immorality of modern warfare as a means of achieving any ultimate good end?

The best part of the call was what the Pope had to say about education for peace: "Men must always speak of peace." ("I think thoughts of peace, and not of affliction, says the Lord.") "The world must be educated to love peace," etc. This, like all education, is an art to be actively pursued, to be practiced in the beginning like finger exercises. It will for most mean hard mental work, because most have habituated themselves to a hopeless cynicism, really a kind of fatalism, on the subject of war. "But there will always be wars; there have always been wars," they say, looking at you blandly. Or, "Do you mean that you wouldn't defend your own life, or your children's?" as though that were the issue here. And even if it were, the pacifist has his answer ready, and it is an impressive one.

Admit the legitimacy of war in modern times and there will always be those who will manage to justify a given war. Such is the magnitude of the task of "educating" for peace. But if there are found in sufficient numbers those who habitually "think thoughts of peace," then there is a more than slender hope for a better world. At the rate we're moving, however, there won't be any world.

I have the convictions needed to qualify as an out-and-out pacifist. I admit, however, that to defend this position I lack the necessary courage. I have never been put in a position physically where I was required to do so; and I go on paying taxes to help support what I am convinced is today a thoroughly immoral war. But I take comfort, because I find I am in very respectable company.

A World's Great Anguish—April 8, 1966

When all has been said that can be said, and written that can be written, who of us can understand just how (we do know why) by the Cross of Christ barriers are cast down, the gulf is crossed, and the arms of the Everlasting Mercy are held out to us? The other day I came upon a passage in an essay on the Atonement by George Tyrell. (Dear, pitiable Tyrell! One wonders how he would be thought of and what his standing would be were he alive today, seeing all that has happened. As for me, I have never doubted where he is!) Let me quote him at some length:

"In every violation of conscience we extinguish some little spark of the divinity that is in us: we eliminate God from our Lives. All sin is some sort of God-murder—'We will not have this man reign over us.' And what each one of us does to that Divine One who, in the midst of our soul, struggles against the godless crowd of our passions and impulses, the same the world may do to the 'just man,' who is to society what conscience is to the individual. Most of all did it seize upon God's dearest and best beloved, upon the Lamb of God, tearing him from limb to limb so that the slain Son of God we see sin revealed and made palpable and visible in its true character. 'This is the heir; let us kill him and the heritage shall be ours.' Of its own nature sin leads eventually to misery and is the poison of human happiness. When man flings himself rebelliously against the adamantine rock of God's will, he but shatters himself to pieces. He intends murder, but effects suicide. But God in his pitying meekness, instead of resisting yields, that the hurt may be all his, and in nowise ours. And this, too, he makes visible to us, in taking to himself the capacity of our humanity to suffer—in which when he might have come down from the cross, he would not. 'When he was reviled, he reviled not again: when he suffered, he threatened not.'"

If I may say this without offense, it seems to me that most American Catholics I know, including my own people and beginning with me, need with almost desperate urgency to acquire a sense of corporate sin. For the sooner we realize our corporate unity with the whole race of men, past and present, the nearer we approach some faint likeness to Christ who bore all the sins and griefs of the world as though they were his own sins and sorrows.

What parent does not blush with shame for the disgrace brought on the family name by an erring son or daughter? What priest does not take personally the discredit brought to the priesthood by an unfaithful fellow-priest? These are familiar emotions everybody understands because they "strike home," as we say. Yet to blush for our common humanity—to make its sins our own, or even more important, to see our own sins as hurting all mankind: somehow this escapes us. Was it not Hawthorne who, appalled by what he saw in a Liverpool workhouse in the mid-1800s said, "I am not clean until the whole world is clean"? That was more than 100 years ago; yet many of us have still to acquire this essentially Christian view of things.

Is it any concern of mine, really, that tens of millions of India are starving? that American Negroes by the millions are debased and defrauded their dignity and their rights? that conscientious objectors and "dissenters" in an allegedly free country are mauled and beaten by a mob while a city's police stand idly by? What concern, indeed, as long as I do not share actively in man's inhumanity to man? The point is, I do share it if only to the extent that I am insensible of it and indifferent to it. Only our Lord was entirely innocent of it.

Tyrrell used an unforgettable phrase to epitomize the Lord's Passion: "Desperate tides," he wrote, "desperate tides of the whole great world's anguish, forced through the channel of a single heart."

'Accepted in the Beloved'—April 22, 1966

A friend has put into my hands an extraordinary little book, *The King in His Beauty*, the text of a short retreat given some years ago by the late Miles Yates, chaplain at the General Theological Seminary in New York. Father Yates was famous for the precision of his spoken and written words, for his mastery of the Mother Tongue. He was a stylist in the best sense of the word. This book is as full of wisdom as it is of literary excellence. I have been using it this Passiontide and Easter.

Yates' meditations on the meaning of Easter are fresh and original. He finds "the word of words" to express God's redeeming work in Christ to be "acceptance"—acceptance in and by the Beloved. What follows here, frankly, is a precis of these glowing pages.

How we prize acceptance! And how necessary it is for our full maturing, this knowledge that our brothers make room for us beside them. (And, we would add, how much pain we cause when we reject others, exile them from our friendship and sympathy.) By how much more, then, are we ennobled and fulfilled by the knowledge that God has "accepted" us. The author suggests that we re-read the Gospels in search of this one theme.

There is, for example, Zacchaeus—that "good but rejected man, forlorn in the sycamore tree." Our Lord was able to read something in this little man's heart as he passed by that day. "Hurry and come down, Zacchaeus; today I must stay in your house." Zacchaeus had found "acceptance" at last. This runt of a man, this pipsqueak, of neither stature nor status stands for any and all of us who are of no account in men's eyes, who couldn't matter less to them, misfits, "rejects," friendless exiles.

There is the woman taken in adultery. Who can forget how gently Christ dealt with her? And she stands for all of us whose sins are chiefly fleshly: the addict and the hapless alcoholic; the homosexual struggling (apparently hopelessly) with his sickness, sensing everywhere but in the comparative security of his own seamy milieu the condemnation, the outright rejection, of his fellow human beings; and hordes and hosts of others, men and women blackballed by the official verdict of society. "No more do I condemn you," says Christ, ". . . let him who is without sin among you cast the first stone."

There is the penitent thief who knew total and final rejection. And to him, "This day you shall be with me in Paradise."

All these, and others we can find for ourselves in the Gospels, had something in them that answered to Christ's tenderness—"an unspoken 'Yes,' a timid and secret orientation Godwards, and there, ready to meet it, was the healing, restorative love of God!

The passage that ends this meditation must stand alone. We give it in full: "We do not earn acceptance before God and with him so that we can claim it as the payment due us, for performance of good or penitence for evil. If what we are has good in it, it also has evil. If what we are has evil in it, it also has good. We cannot present a pure offering, an unmixed oblation of right thoughts and acts to God; we can only want to be and do our best, in response to his love. But once, in our manhood, the pure offering, the unmixed oblation, was lifted up from earth to heaven in the manhood of our Lord; and our least 'Yes' to it brings us the clasp of the outstretched hand. Forgiveness, reconciliation, acceptance for the man-as-he-is: imperfect, in the making, ignorant or discerning, innocent or guilty—conditional only on that inward, right-about-face that turns the soul to God. We are 'accepted in the Beloved' not for the poor results of our efforts, but from the compassion of infinite love. Not because of our worth, but in spite of our unworth."

Plain Talk About Marriage—November 19, 1965

This is how Simon and Schuster, its publishers, describe Robert Farrar Capon's *Bed and Board*. So "plain" indeed, and so enlightening, is this "talk" that a celibate like me, I feel, has now no business to say a word about marriage unless and until he has read, marked, learned, and inwardly digested every word of it. I have read and reread it and urged my people, especially all fathers, to go and do likewise.

The author is described as "an Episcopal priest, player of music, teacher of Greek, husband, father of six." He is vicar of a small parish on Long Island's north shore as well as dean of a seminary for delayed vocations established recently by the Diocese of Long Island. This latter, I am told, is handsomely endowed. If this is so, then one may assume that Father Capon is not, as is the clergy in general, underpaid for his talents. That this, too, may make it a trifle easier for him to talk plainly about marriage, I strongly suspect. The only fact I have, however, is that he enjoys both bed and board in a large, "rambling old house, amid sea breezes, ensemble music, and the aroma" of *la haute cuisine*. Marriage under these conditions is surely an easier pursuit than it is for men who pay through the nose for small packing-boxes they and their families will outgrow in less than ten years' time. I have to get this off my chest, for the falling of Father Capon's lines in extremely pleasant places seems to me to set him apart from millions of urban and suburban American—and English, and French, and West German, and Italian—fathers. How can a man raise a large family Christianly without money—not wealth, but money enough—and ample living space? Even so, *Bed and Board* is required reading for its humanity and humor, for its wisdom and wit, for its sense and sensibility. Read it and give it to your friends to read.

Pay close attention to what this husband has to say about *BED*—about the difference between SEX (something dirty) and SEXUALITY (something godly and glorious); about the proper role and function of the man as "head of the wife" and her always courtly lover; about the chastity that is proper to true marriage.

Read and read again and again what he has to say about "caring," by which he means learning to do something lovingly and well, whether it is playing the recorder or making a soufflé or cultivating a taste of good wines. See how he teaches his children to "care."

Listen to him talk about his children and watch him as he looks at them in open delight and wonder (for, says he, "You will never see their like again."). "Be their Teacher," he counsels, "and expect a lot from them." Love them, fathers, with self-giving, with humor, with small talk, with "the minor affections of your hands and eyes." And once again, "Delight in them openly." I should not for anything have missed these pages nor the sheer poetry of the apostrophes he addresses to them, one by one, near the end of the book. These are purest gold, I think. Most fathers can feel like this, but few there are who can put what they feel into words. What a legacy to leave your children!

Father Capon will, I feel, bear me no ill will if, in closing this little review of his very great book, I have this to say: I should like a sequel to *Bed and Board*. But I should like Mrs. Capon to write it!

But Where is the Action?—July 21, 1967

A young layman remarked to me the other day: "I had to make a delivery one mid-morning last week to one of the convents in the area. I went into the chapel and there, kneeling on the pavement with her arms extended to form a cross, was a young religious. Why wasn't she somewhere else at that hour of the day doing something important, making herself useful?"

It is an old, old question. Novices rebel these days, they tell us, against a regimen that promotes "personal sanctification" at the expense of "service." Religious, especially the women, seek escape from their "nunny little world" to go where the action is. But are the issues quite so sharply drawn as all that? Is the alternative necessarily so radical? Has prayer, truly understood, even been merely passive, its fruits wholly subjective? Certainly not. Is not prayer, rather, the beginning, the first step, in all action that is truly Christian? We know that it is.

One of my friends of the old days, having taken his degree at Harvard and done his service in World War II, went off to England to prepare for receiving Anglican Orders. After three years he was convinced that the cloistered life was his true vocation. He sought in vain among the Anglican religious communities abroad for one that would answer his need. Over here he looked to the Order of the Holy Cross, where one of the men was about to try living in a hermitage on the community's property and was told that in the American Episcopal Church there was really no place for the contemplative life. So my friend "went over" to Rome forthwith, became a Trappist monk, and after solemn profession was ordained a priest. His point was that no church could claim to be Catholic or even to be a "part" of the Catholic Church that failed to provide for the contemplative life. Is he wasting his life today? Ought he today to be where the action is? I do not think so. Does he, I wonder? All I know is the three most exciting places I know today are Mount Saviour, Spencer, and Montfort in our own nearby Litchfield. (I do not know Taizé, save by hearsay.)

Thomas Merton in his more recent books insists that contemplation is the mark of the fully mature Christian. He does not demand that the contemplative live in a community of contemplatives. Nor need he be a hermit, a Christian Thoreau. Any man can be a contemplative, and in a sense must be if he would be full-grown according to the measure of the stature of the complete man, Christ. But Merton also insists that the Christian life flowers only as it serves, only as it lays itself down without reserve in the service of others. The "new man in Christ" has always been both friend and son of God, and friend and brother of men.

Cloistered, active, or "mixed"—there have been the traditional forms take by religious communities in the past, and men and women have made their choices accordingly. But are the lines so clearly drawn today? They need not be; they should not be, in my view. The Church cannot afford to lose any of the myriad goods peculiar to each of these types of life. Yet while preserving these, every religious community can and should so revise and reform its life—rule, habit, ways of worship, and particular "works"—as unfailingly to make its impress on the contemporary world. When they do, they will have escaped the charge of irrelevance, and not until. When they do, there will be vocations aplenty. For if ever a sick and tortured world needed the religious community, it is today!

'Accept, O Lord, My Memory'—February 18, 1965

Almost everyone is familiar with the "Suscipe" attributed to St. Ignatius which begins with the words of our title. Memory, understanding, and will are entrusted to the healing and restorative power of God, and this is the first and necessary step in the total offering of oneself at the beginning of each new day. We shall look at the first of the three, the memory.

How often have you found it hard to pray when all you could think of was your wretchedness, your past sins and then memory of them? Try as you would to think of God, to free yourself from yourself in his presence, you could not evade the accusing finger of conscience, nor escape the haunting memory of sin. How poor must have been the Prodigal's appetite at that great dinner! The best robe could only have reminded him of the filth he has wallowed in; and how unsavory must the roast lamb have been in his mouth! The memory of sin can often quite obscure, for a time, even the joy we take in the sure knowledge of our heavenly Father's love. Yet this is not meant to be. The Father's forgiveness was without reserve, limitless. It was the son's remorse that stood in the way of full and free acceptance. Is there healing for this spiritual uneasiness, in the presence of infinite love? There is. It is the practice of reparation.

For it is one of the uses of reparation to help us make up for the time lost, for injuries done, for opportunities thrown away, for love sighted. Like the Prodigal, we come to ourselves, seeing ourselves, as we are. Not liking what we seem, we rise up and go to confession, and only then can we really undertake to repair the damage done. We do our penance. And, for our own sakes, we ask God at the same time to heal and then to hallow our tormented memory. This is rarely, if ever, done overnight. Some men have spent a lifetime in reparation. All of us need every day to say, "Accept, O Lord, my memory . . ."

"But," someone is sure to say, "how can the trivial penance I am given possibly fulfill my reparation?" It cannot, of course, in and of itself. No penance can, even the longest and hardest. I remember a woman who, during the Holy Year, determined to go to Rome as a penitent. She planned to make a life confession in the hope that she might be given a severe penance and thus to her satisfaction make up for a frivolous and worldly life. As we listened to her plans, we saw visions of hard stone stairways toilsomely climbed on blistered knees, of innumerable ways of the Cross trod by this bedraggled penitent. The prospect was faintly amusing to her friends as she pictured it. Imagine her surprise when the old confessor in Rome gave her "Three Hail Marys," was the reply. "Go in peace."

It is precisely this rude contrast between the lightness of our penance and the weight of our sins that shows us that some greater reparation is needed, greater by far than any we can make, if the righteousness of God is to be satisfied. Our trivial penances, our haunting memories, become infinite in value only when they are added to the reparation Christ made for us. We forget that *he* is our confession, *he* is our sorrow, *he* our only penance, and *he* our reparation.

So if the memory of your sins and the consciousness of your sinfulness come between God and yourself, the way to God through the cloud of that memory and the wasteland of self-knowledge is the way of reparation.

Learn to make an act of reparation each day, not simply when a penance is given you, but every day and many times a day. Take on some small penance, some hard thing, every day simply to develop the habit of reparation. Soon—sooner than we think now—we shall discover that the light of God's love will lighten our own darkness and deliver us from the perils of our night of sin.

There is one more point to make in this matter. It is one thing, as we know, to make up to God; but suppose there is no way now of reaching someone you've injured. Suppose, long ago, you did something to hurt somebody, and that person is now beyond your reach. First of all, the very suffering itself that you feel can be offered as your reparation. The glorious thing about the Church is that we are one body and members one of another. The injured friend may be four thousand miles away, or he may be dead; but you are still one with him in the Church, one with him in Christ. Any reparation you do in name of Jesus; the penance you accept from the Church; the sorrow and shame you are willing to bear; all these will have their part in undoing the injury. Prayer and penance will help those beyond our reach. As for you, put your troubled conscience at rest and leave the past to God.

It's a Well-Calculated Risk—July 7, 1967

Much is being said and written today, much indeed in the highest places, about the layman's importance and his increasing responsibility in the life of the Church. Some have gone so far as to call this the age of the layman. If it is, it is not because we have begun to use the layman at his fullest capacity but because his priests are coming to see that they cannot without his help adequately do their real job. This is a beginning only, but it is our view, a good one.

It is no new experience to us, this recruiting of lay help in the work of the Church. The American Episcopal Church is so organized that its laymen serve on parish "vestries", as they are called; in fact, with the rector they are in law the parish corporation. They constitute one of the two houses—the lower, so to speak, of lay delegates—of each diocesan convention meeting annually with the bishop and clergy to run the church's business. They "call" their clergyman and have a voice in the election of their bishops.

This way of doing things we learned over the years to accept despite manifold annoyances. All the dangers of "trusteeism," all the frustrations of the democratic process were latent in the system and sometimes these were real and actual. Yet, all in all, its merits outweighed its defects, for it insured a responsible, informed, and working laity. We have called this a well-calculated risk, and so it is; but it need not be insurmountable nor beyond discreet control.

The secret of success we found to be the clear-cut distinction between the temporalities and the spiritualities. Charged with the latter, we allowed no encroachment. Yet dependent as we were on lay help in the temporalities, we felt free to accept or reject suggestions.

But consider how invaluable was this help when there were seven lawyers on the vestry, a very astute businessman, and one C.P.A. who for years was parish treasurer. These men were the people's representatives on the parish council; yet even the people had their say at the annual parish meeting when elections were held, a budget was presented and voted on, and a complete and detailed financial statement was submitted. Sometimes these occasions were harrowing, but we lived through them. Given the system, a vast give-and-take, and mutual trust and confidence, parish life was in the long run the sounder and more vigorous for it.

There are those among us who are afraid of an outbreak of "trusteeism," just as there are among us a few who want the layman to have his say about everything. The latter might find it useful to consult with their Congregational minister-friends who (it would appear to us) cannot so much as replace a burned-out light bulb without the permission of the Board of Deacons! No, somewhere in the middle lies the safest course. The fact is, to our average intelligent layman the Church is something very dear; it is "his business" and he should have a real and responsible role in its administration. We shall be all the better when his brains, his energies and skills, and his goodwill are brought to bear on the active life of every parish.

Dearly Beloved Physician—September 20, 1962

It was something to experience and to remember, the funeral of a much beloved physician. The colorful parish church well filled, scores of the reverend clergy, the brother-priest who offered the Mass, the choir of religious, the sisters, and fellow doctors; all of these by their presence that morning testified to their affection, their respect, and doubtless their gratitude to God and through him to his doctor whose career of singular service and devotion death had so untimely brought to a close.

Above all, in this tender human scene of restrained sorrow, there was the gallant family. Here, it seemed to me, as I worshipped with the mother and her magnificent sons, was an example of faith at its highest, of serene courage at its noblest, of deep devotion at its strongest.

Where will you find except in the devoted priest and pastor any man as Christlike as the good doctor? I do not insist on the *Christian* doctor, you will notice, for I have known and know many Jewish doctors who have this stamp. Anyway, my thoughts that morning turned naturally to my own father whose disappointment at my not choosing to follow in his steps was hidden by his words to me, "You have chosen the better part. There are physicians of the souls, and theirs is the more important work." That is why I have never doubted that the good doctor comes second only to the priest in the ranks of high service to mankind. The wise man, the teacher who hands on the truth to others, comes third and this trinity helps us keep "the whole law and the prophets," the love of God and the love of neighbor.

Spoiled as I am by the best. I ask of my doctor, as do many of you, that understanding and concern which make of his service to me a true ministry. Like my priest, he must be the kind of man to whom my life is an open book. And whereas his skill, his cold objectivity, are essential to my physical well-being, medical science is increasingly aware of the equally essential element of a close, an almost pastoral relation, between doctor and patient. My doctor is numbered among my closest friends. Is this a burden on him? Of course it is; but it is one he will gladly bear because he is the good physician. Thus, any program of "Medicare" which deprives me of this unique blessing, the boon of my doctor's friendship, is, I should suppose, to be resisted.

Thinking of the great doctors I know and have known, I take fresh inspiration from their example of total dedication. All too often have they and do they put me to shame. It is a truism that their wives and children share them with the public. Oftentimes it is you and I who claim the larger share. Let the young man who tell you he is "going into medicine to make money" beware: he will never be really happy nor will he be a great doctor. This was not what made the Oslers and the Schweitzers and the Dooleys great, for theirs was a solemn vocation to service. Theirs was a true ministry to the whole man—to soul as well as to body.

Young Man with Conscience—January 21, 1966

Thomas Lyons is in his late twenties or early thirties. He teaches at Phillips Andover. His great love is American history. Of distinctly scholarly bent, he is nonetheless a skilled teacher of boys. I have only the slightest acquaintance with him, having met him in a social way three years ago when he was on the faculty of Mount Hermon. Reading the current issues of the Andover alumni bulletin, I realized not only what Andover has to gain in a man like Lyons, but how vastly changed the Andover of our day is from the school I knew. I should add that Lyons is a victim of polio. Despite his very considerable physical handicap, he coaches intramural football. I have seen him working with his team, lying on his back at the sidelines; I have seen his boys lift him and carry him to his car after practice. This was pretty impressive, as you may well imagine, and this by no means minor detail may account, if not for his brilliance, then certainly for his compassion for the suffering. Here is a man tried every day, and every moment of the day, in the school of pain. The alumni bulletin carries this month an address this young man made at a recent conference on the "culturally deprived" student and Andover's responsibility to him. Unfortunately, space here permits only the briefest resume.

Andover, Lyons contends, and schools like it—independent schools of top quality and, I should myself add, our own best Catholic high schools and boarding schools—should seek "to broaden the socioeconomic, cultural, racial, and ethnic composition of the student body." This, he says, is demanded by our national security, that is, if we wish to find constructive outlets for our current social tensions and if we would prevent their exploding into chaos. Our better schools must take the lead now, since it will require years before our urban public education can deal with the "talented tenth," as Andover and schools like it can do at once. The independent school is free (or ought to be free) from the social and political pressures and the public apathy that all too often interfere with the educational process.

Although the independent school can hope to reach only a few of the 20 million American Negroes or the 40 million American poor, it must nevertheless do all it can—and this if for no other reason than that it will contribute as much to the conventional student body as it will for the exceptional student. The independent school must open its doors; it must assume leadership; it must at all cost avoid the "conventional wisdom" which may in the end be folly; it must confront today's realities not tomorrow, but today.

Best of all is his last reason: "We should so commit ourselves because it is socially and morally right to do so."

He follows this plea with a brilliant excursus on the "culturally deprived" adolescent. This is one of the most enlightening analyses of this "alien, not radical" American that I have ever come upon. These few paragraphs—pure gold in my mind—should have far wider notice than they are likely to gain from their appearance in the alumni bulletin.

Lyons, however, is not through yet. He has recommendations for the composition of the school's faculty. "I propose," he says, "a more catholic faculty in geographic, ethnic, religious, racial, educational, and socioeconomic background. Are we not too heavily weighted with Andover alumni, Ivy Leaguers, and white Anglo-Saxon Protestants?"

The reaction to all this? Wouldn't you know it? The Old Guard didn't like it. Tough, isn't it?

'The Dear, Tired Sisters'—June 21, 1962

Early in my priesthood I was invited to speak to the graduates of a parish school. This was for me an entirely new experience and knowing nothing of etiquette and procedure on these occasions. I asked what was expected of me. The young priest I consulted told me how to begin—the greetings and how to word them and in what order. "And don't forget," he added, "the dear, tired sisters."

We have all been concerned these past few weeks, and will be for some time to come, with the unique place and role of Catholic education in America, and now, in mid-month, with thousands of our boys and girls and young men and young women who staff the greater number of them; yet there is, I think, the danger that we take these devoted teachers for granted.

We ought, for example, to consider by what astronomical number the cost of Catholic education, already heavy to bear, would increase were it not for this body of absolutely dedicated teachers whose only desire is to serve. They are the marvel, let me assure you, of our non-Catholic friends who, whatever the limits of their understanding of our religious, are quite aware of the magnificent example and devotion of these women. For our teaching sisters ask nothing but the high privilege of working hard and tirelessly—nothing, that is, but the bare necessities of life: suitable shelter, the simplest of fare, a chapel waxed to a perilous degree and kept shining and bright for the divine Guest, and the opportunity during the summers of studying and improving their skills. My own view is that nothing is too good for them, neither trouble we could take for them nor expense we could bear on their behalf. They should not have to struggle to meet budgets or to find money on their own for the necessary expansion of their many good works and the needs of their communities. We should, because we could so easily, shower them with our gifts of money and leave them free from worry.

I well know that these women are human and have, therefore, their shortcomings. But I must say this: never have I seen these betrayed by outward behavior. You know that I mean: patience under the most trifling and maddening of interruptions; a smile to greet yet another task imposed at a long day's end; meticulous doing of what has to be done, often over and beyond strict duty, which is another way of saying that we too often impose on them; impeccable manners, which are passed on and become second nature to our boys and girls; sweet courtesy, habitual good humor, and not infrequently genuine joy. Have you watched them when you have praised them? Is it possible that their pleasure is the keener because we take thought to praise them so rarely?

I have so far confined my tribute to our teaching sisters. But this is not to forget those who nurse the sick, who take care of our seminaries, who look after me, for example. Nor is it to overlook the contemplatives, those whose life is altogether prayer and praise and reparation. Can you imagine the household of Faith, the Church of Christ, without them? I can't.

The Indispensable Parish—October 25, 1968

I do not mean the indispensable parish *church*, the *building* as such. It can be a rented hall, a school auditorium, a grassy hillside under certain conditions, a catacomb or its modern equivalent. I mean only some place where a roof can be put over a table and under which people can be gathered in and sheltered from the elements. I do not care even if you prefer nor to call it a church.

Those among us who advocate the scrapping of familiar and time-tested ways in parish life are overlooking, it seems to me, an important group of people and are doing them, unwittingly, much injury. A few weeks ago, and in a context slightly different from mine, Rosemary Ruether spoke to this point when she observed that in so many parishes these days drastic external changes are made and much that once was a familiar is stripped away, but that little is provided in their place. The people are bewildered, especially the aging and the aged, she said; and she is right.

I have heard priests who should know better speak contemptuously of the "pious old ladies" who attend the weekday Mass. Scorn is heaped on the guilds and societies. "Purely private religion," "noninvolved Christianity so-called"—these are expressions I have heard. I am offended by them, but what is worse, I know that somewhere, somehow, the devout, too, are being hurt if only by being passed over and forgotten. These priests are for the most part very young.

What they do not realize is that people grow old; that there are persons in large numbers who have dug roots and who cherish and nurture their roots; that many stay put and would sooner die, literally, than be exiled from the familiar; that these are too old to take part in demonstrations and fight boldly and publicly for important causes; that they are nor perhaps up to reading the most important books; that for these the parish church is "home" in perhaps the truest sense of that word.

My "pious" or "devout"—however you describe them—happen, oddly enough, to be old men. Four are retired; one, in his mid-80s, drives "through ice, mud, and snow" a distance of five miles to be at Mass every day. Indeed, my men are not all elderly: two young fathers bring their sons, four little boys in all, to Mass daily. And always, standing about the altar, the males—old, not so old, and very young—outnumber the women. I am rather proud of this fact.

One elderly man, a founding father of my parish 25 years ago, tells me that as a boy he used to walk from South Windsor to East Hartford every Sunday to church. He has recently lost his wife. The early morning she was taken to the hospital, he on his way back home stopped at the church and stayed through Mass. He and his son were there the next morning. The following day death occurred early, and the two were back again to tell me the news and to stay for Mass.

This may be awfully "old hat" and totally "unrelated" to our world, but somehow I am still moved by it. What are the young and activist priests doing to prepare the people for the day of *individual* crisis, those that tell us "you only know God through people?" Where could such courage and resignation have all these years been prepared for and now be sustained; where developed this kind of life-time devotion; if not in and through the ministry of a parish church?

For these persons the parish church is a sign of stability and continuity in a totally disoriented and bewildering and frightening world. And where could such as these go for help but where they have always sought it—from the parish priest in the familiar parish church?

7

For Modern America

A Conclusion

Yes, "For Modern America" as in "for the American Christian churches of today": Catholic, Protestant, and Orthodox. I trust readers are not left wondering why a decade's worth of Catholic newspaper columns from the 1960s deserve reflection, and even fulfillment, in the 2020s. Surely Gordon made the case that ecumenism is essential for the Church as the Body of Christ; but the trials and tribulations of yesterday have evolved into the present near impasse. His passion for reform took him much further than Anglo-Catholics before or since: home and interfaith Eucharists with all of the essential reverence and devotion but little of the formality. Some of the formality should live on, nevertheless, in larger gatherings of the faithful, where there is always the need for beauty, at times grandeur, in celebration, architecture, and music. Engagement with the biblical books, along with interpretation renewed by contemporary historical research and literary refinement, has seldom been so clearly promoted as in these columns, as useful for readers in the 2020s as decades ago. And the many connections he makes between self-examining spirituality and participation in the Church's mission, while often responses to the crises of the 1960s, are obviously not time-bound by that era. Thus we have his themes: the ideas and the specific vision he gave voice to. Now to take them one by one in conclusion.

The Great Church and Ecumenism

The Great Church that is coming into being *is* the risen body of Christ, and so the Anglo-Catholic experience across the years must be grounded in ecumenism, the reuniting of all members. Mourning the multiple separations will lead to venturing prayers and conversations together, which will then lead to the more beautiful ceremonial moments. There will be isolated liturgical celebrations when Catholics, Protestants, and Anglicans achieve a union that is not generally doable: intercommunion. These moments are not to be condemned but are to be seen as the early arrival of the future realities.

An Anglo-Catholic of the Roman obedience at first rejoices in a personal conversion experience and yearns for others to join, but this gives way to appreciating more and more the accomplishments of Protestantism, especially in humble service (Methodism) and in a missionary apostolate to the poor in the cities at home and the colonial countryside (Anglicanism). At the ideal spiritual moment, the Anglo-Catholic in the Great Church will stay put and work from within, because this Church, the body of Christ, is built up by love, witness, and unceasing ecumenical efforts.

The Liturgy: Tradition and Acculturation

The Eucharist is the pre-eminent gathering together of the members of the Great Church; the more members faithful to the gathering, the more alive it is, the more will the faithful be changed and renewed. Physical presence, voice, movement are the realities of engagement of the whole person. Prayer and ceremonial are not to be encumbered by trivia. The essence of Eucharist is a meal embodied best in the home Eucharist—where families and friends can feel and know they are at the Lord's banquet table. In other settings such as schools and camps, priest and people must appropriately recreate the Last Supper. Always, of course, there is a dialogue, account of the Last Supper, remembrance of Christ's life, passion, death, resurrection, ascension, and the calling down of the Holy Spirit. Creating the ideal Eucharistic Prayer is work in progress, but any liturgy will fail if rushed and irreverent—so often the case.

Broad challenges remain, to rework the death and burial liturgies, revise translations, and provide the right physical settings. Unadorned churches where the altar of sacrifice, ambo for proclaiming scripture, reservation tabernacle, and baptismal font—all these—have an American prototype in a Connecticut Episcopal church, with its high altar, great screen behind the altar, and stained glass that proclaims, "O all ye works of the lord, bless ye the Lord." The new Catholic churches of Europe in their simplicity also facilitate the interplay between liturgical prayer and physical setting. Finally, musical simplicity mediates, as should all elements of the liturgy, between tradition and acculturation.

The Bible for Everyone

The epistles of Paul are the pre-eminent New Testament interpretation of the death and resurrection of Christ, and Paul invokes the Spirit as the source of Christian sharing, often through suffering, in his experience. The suffering of Job, recounted in the biblical book of the same name, is the message for all of us that God's ways are mysterious and that positive thinking is not a viable shortcut to understanding them. Praying the psalms, then, becomes the best option, for here one enters through Hebrew poetry into the mystery of Christ's suffering and into the daily life of the church.

For the most down-to-earth of the gospels, one might well begin with St. Luke: tender human stories such as Christ's infancy, Martha and Mary, Zacchaeus the tax collector, and the parables of the prodigal son and the good Samaritan. Assimilation of the parables, more important than anything more dramatic such as speaking in tongues, depends upon an existential reading experience, unfettered by either evangelical commentaries or the overheated metaphorical interpretations of the church fathers. Thus, bible study, beyond literalist readings and proof texting, is a saving grace for all Christians, nowhere more than in conjunction with the church year, which celebrates the mysteries of Christ's life, death, resurrection, and ascension. We come to know the self-emptying of God at Christmas, the mystery of death on Good Friday, and the triumphant resurrection and ascension. Bible study in the end opens us up to a vision of Christ the King over all.

Spiritual Life and Christian Mission

There is no spiritual life without Christian mission. Bystanders, on their own or together as citizens of a nation, are, then, guilty: nowhere more than when promoting war. Repentance is a beginning, and much is learned here from the suffering for justice visible in the lives of black Americans young and old, of pacifists, and of those who accept their neighbors, whatever their qualities. Acceptance of others is also the key to self-acceptance.

Spiritual life enhances a marriage, from mutual devotion of the spouses, through delighting in kids, to the pleasures of bed and board.

Religious communities, whether they be cloistered, in the active apostolate, or mixed, can invigorate the spiritual lives of their members and the people they serve. But in the end all are sinners, so those that are haunted by their sins should seek the way of reparation out of their darkness.

Vocation, the work of a lifetime, such as the doctor's or the teacher's, is salvific for others. At the heroic levels seen in the lives of missionary doctors, self-sacrificing young teachers, and the Catholic sisters that manage so many schools and hospitals, vocation becomes Christian mission. Ultimately, the grounding of this mission is the home parish or community.

In Fine

The lifelong Anglo-Catholic vocation of Gordon Wadhams was marked by inspiring family experiences, enlivened by his own youthful experiments with churchgoing, and focused by his friends and mentors, Episcopal and Catholic. His timeline is not our own, but it serves as a template for our own search to understand how the great church is built up by ecumenism, how its liturgy develops by acculturation of timeless traditions, how it valorizes the biblical writings for each generation and guarantees a living spirituality to all believers by pressing on with its divinely commissioned apostolate.

Appendix

A Personal Note

Not that I have been a disinterested observer.

At several key moments in my life, "Father Wadhams," as professor and preacher, gave me new confidence in and heightened hope for my own formation and apostolate. I first met him when I was a student at the St. Thomas archdiocesan minor seminary in Bloomfield, Connecticut. Back then it was the custom for priest faculty members to celebrate their own private masses each day. They would descend at their scheduled times into a basement chapel with multiple altars, and to each one was assigned a seminarian acolyte. Serving Gordon's mass, I noted his care for each gesture, each genuflection, his quiet, unhurried Latin. That is how mass must be prayed, I thought. Back above ground, later in the day, it was first-year college French, with Gordon's help at pronunciation, composition, and appreciation of the literature. Molière's *Les Fourberies de Scapin* never ceased to amuse him, chuckling every time the quirky line "Que diable allait-il faire dans cette galère" ["What the hell was he doing in that galley ship"] came by. To be brief, the roguish Scapin had convinced the father of a principal character that his son while traveling in a sea galley had been captured by Turkish pirates, and that he, Scapin, could deliver the ransom money. The father wanted to rustle up the money, but couldn't figure why his son was so traveling in the first place. It was a nonsensical play for sure.

One of the few professors to never wander from the subject matter, Gordon would nevertheless quickly comment on the remarkable liturgical value of *The Church's Year of Grace* by Pius Parsch or on the successful elements of our French essays as we read them in class or even random French cultural details such as the healthy privacy of the showers at the French lycée where he had taught for a year after graduating from college! And with some regularity across that semester he would say, "one wonders what Peter Rosazza is doing these days," because one of his former students had just headed to the major seminary of the Archdiocese of Paris, Saint-Sulpice, for the final years of priestly formation (Ordained in Notre-Dame cathedral, Father Rosazza returned to Connecticut, eventually becoming the auxiliary bishop for the Hispanic apostolate—to Gordon's great satisfaction.) Knowing that we seminarians had little interest in current affairs, he would urge regular newspaper reads, adding "and by 'newspaper' I mean the *New York Times.*"

Six years later at the major seminary of the Montfort Fathers in Litchfield, Gordon came by once a week to teach preaching. And so, in the last year before ordination, I experienced his affable and encouraging comments—all the more memorable to me when he afterwards told the seminary rector in an aside, "I was moved, Father, by Joseph Byrnes's homily; I was moved." My many preaching years after this were buoyed up by the confidence he had instilled in me. But he could be funny, too, with his preaching anecdotes: the lively Scottish-accented lady who said of a sermon, "'Twas read, 'twas badly read, 'twasn't worth the readin'," or the New York parishioner who liked an Old Testament reference to the Medes and Parthians because, "my mother was a Mead, you know." Gordon would also quite politely reformulate our simple remarks evaluating one another's homilies: so, to a "There was no meat and potatoes" comment Gordon responded, "Yes, lacked substance" and continued on similarly, translating fairly hapless remarks into worthwhile observations.

With all of this, I dared to invite him to preach the homily at my first parish mass after ordination, and he accepted immediately. Although this was almost sixty years ago, and in spite of my nervousness then, I remember his quote from his old mentor, the Benedictine abbot Damasus Winzen: "Priesthood is like a loaf of bread which God the Father shares with his children." Even more important, perhaps, was the reflection quoted in the Waterbury newspaper report the next day." The crowning virtue of a priest is charity towards all people" with special "compassion for the wayward, for the ignorant" I shouldn't have been surprised, then, when he dedicated a column to an article I published in the Jesuit magazine *America* less than two years later, "How Far is Up: On Updating the Clergy." It was a prolonged reflection on ministering in a time of renewal delayed by the resistance in the congregation and the slow pace of official reform.

Would that I had contacted him soon—or any time—after that. But I did not: working in another part of the country, doing graduate work at the University of Chicago, and eventually resigning from the clergy because I wanted to have a family. Somehow I didn't take seriously enough the comment of my hometown pastor, who told me that Gordon was finding his retirement years difficult. Of his death and funeral I was uninformed. So it was with relief and joy that I came upon his last column while preparing this anthology. Along with his typical appreciation of young priests, he commented that celibacy was an unjust requirement for priestly ordination, in fact damaging for the church, and something he would *not* have himself embraced if he had it to do over again. The memory of his father, Dr. Noah Wadhams, married and dedicated to his patients more than most celibate priests to their people, was Gordon's inspiration to the end, perhaps as much as was John Henry Newman.

Bibliography

Ackerman, Keith. "The Changing World of Anglo-Catholicism." Virtue Online. https://virtueonline.org/changing-world-anglo-catholicism.

Allport, Gordon W. *The Individual and His Religion: A Psychological Interpretation*. New Haven: Yale University Press, 1955.

Brown, Stewart J., Peter B. Nockles, and James Perreiro, eds. *The Oxford Handbook of the Oxford Movement*. Oxford: Oxford University Press, 2017.

Cameron, J. M. "John Henry Newman and the Tractarian Movement." In *Nineteenth Century Religious Thought in the West*, Ninian Smart et al., eds. 3 vols. New York: Cambridge University Press, 1985.

"Catholic Transcript, 1960–1969." Catholic Research Resources Alliance. https://thecatholicnewsarchive.org.

Chadwick, Owen. *The Victorian Church*. 2 vols., 3rd ed. London: Adam and Charles Black, 1971.

Dawley, Powel Mills. *The Story of General Theological Seminary: A Sesquicentennial History, 1917–1967*. New York: Oxford University Press, 1969.

DeMille, George E. *The Catholic Movement in the American Episcopal Church*. Eugene, OR: Wipf & Stock, 2006.

Dix, Gregory. *The Shape of the Liturgy*. London: Dacre Press, 1949.

Fairbairn, A. M. *Catholicism: Roman and Anglican*. London: Houghton & Stoughten, 1899.

Ker, Ian. *John Henry Newman: A Biography*. New York: Oxford University Press, 1988.

Pickering, W. S. F. *Anglo-Catholicism: A Study in Religious Ambiguity*. London: SPCK, 1989.

Rowell, Geoffrey. *The Vision Glorious: Themes and Personalities of the Catholic Revival in Anglicanism*. New York: Oxford University Press, 1983.

Stowe, Walter Herbert. *Anglo-Catholicism: What It Is Not and What It Is*. London: Church Literature Association, 1932. http://anglicanhistory.org/usa/whstowe/what1932.html.

Stevens, Harriet Weeks Wadhams. *Wadhams Genealogy, Preceded by a Sketch of the Wadhams Family in England.* New York: Frank Allaben Genealogical Company, 1913. Forgotten Books Reprint, 2018.
Yelton, Michael. *Anglo Papalism: An Illustrated History.* London: Canterbury Press, 2005.

Printed by BoD™in Norderstedt, Germany